Pittsburgh Series in Bibliography

NELSON ALGREN

Nelson Algren

Photo by Stephen Deutch

Nelson Algren

A DESCRIPTIVE BIBLIOGRAPHY

Matthew J. Bruccoli

with the assistance of Judith Baughman

UNIVERSITY OF
PITTSBURGH PRESS
1985

For Michael and Kathleen Lazare

Published by the University of Pittsburgh Press, Pittsburgh, Pa. 15260
Copyright © 1985, University of Pittsburgh Press
All rights reserved
Feffer and Simons, Inc., London
Manufactured in the United States of America

Library of Congress Cataloging in Publication Data

Bruccoli, Matthew Joseph, 1931–
  Nelson Algren: a descriptive bibliography.

  (Pittsburgh series in bibliography)
  1. Algron, Nelson 1909–1981.—Bibliography.
I. Baughman, Judith. II. Title. III. Series.
Z8027.16.B78 1985   [PS3501.L4625]   016.813'52   85-1180
ISBN 0-8229-3517-1 (alk. paper)

Contents

Acknowledgments

ALL good bibliographies are collaborations. I am indebted to the following: Rose Adkins, *Writer's Digest;* James Ahearn, *Bergen Record;* Shaye Areheart and William Koch, Doubleday; Betty B. Bandy; Matt Brook; Edward P. J. Corbett, Ohio State University; Mark Dolan; Candida Donadio; James Hardin, University of South Carolina; Daniel Henson; Jan Herman; Lawrence Hill; Peter Howard, Serendipity Books; Fred Kleeberg; Inge Kutt; Jay Landesman; William Matheson, Elsie M. Maylott, and Leonard N. Beck, Library of Congress; Roger Mortimer, Thomas Cooper Library, University of South Carolina; Michael Mullen; Melvin New, University of Florida; Andrew Patner and Christine Newman, *Chicago;* David Ray; Tim Schobert, Morisset Library, University of Ottawa; Richard Studing, Wayne State University; Douglas Swartz; Rodger Tarr, Illinois State University; Arthur Wang; Ian Willison, British Library; Mary Wolf, Wolf-Mills Music. Kenneth G. McCollum and Linda Oxley provided extraordinary assistance. Paul and Elizabeth Garon of Beasley Books checked this bibliography; they rescued me from at least two blunders, provided new entries, and generously lent material from their collection, which is now in the Chicago Public Library. The Library of Congress, the U.S. Copyright Office, and the British Library are always good places to work.

Kenneth Toombs, Director of the Thomas Cooper Library, and Professor Trevor Howard-Hill arranged for the University of South Carolina to acquire the Algren core collection from which I worked. My greatest obligation is to the long-suffering Interlibrary Loan staff at the Cooper Library: Harriet Oglesbee, Daniel Boice, Lori Finger, Jan Squire, Susan Bradley, Dana Rabon.

The University of South Carolina makes it possible for me to get my work done; and I am particularly grateful to Professor George Geckle, Chairman of the Department of English, for his support.

Mary Bruccoli and Joseph Caldwell did the photographic work.

My working draft was vetted by William Cagle, Charles Mann, and Joel Myerson. I am grateful to Jane Flanders of the University of Pittsburgh Press for giving the setting copy its final editing. Frederick A. Hetzel, Director of the Press, has made this series possible.

Introduction

PUBLICATION is the essential act of scholarship, but all bibliographies are works in progress.

FORMAT

Section A lists chronologically all books and pamphlets by Nelson Algren, including all printings of all editions in English. The numbering system for Section A designates the edition and printing for each entry. Thus for the first English printing of *Never Come Morning,* A 2.1.b indicates that the volume described is the second book by Algren (A 2) and that it is the second printing of the first edition (1.b). Issues are designated by subscripts: A 4.1.a$_2$ indicates the signed issue of the first printing of *The Man With the Golden Arm.*

Section B lists chronologically the first publication in books and pamphlets of material by Algren. Previous periodical appearances of these items are stipulated. In most cases, only the first printings of B entries are described.

Section C lists chronologically the first appearances of Algren contributions, exclusive of reviews, in magazines and newspapers.

Section D lists chronologically the reviews by Algren in magazines and newspapers.

Section E lists blurbs by Algren in books and ads.

Appendix 1 contains the compiler's notes.

Appendix 2 lists books and bibliographical articles about Algren.

TERMS AND METHODS

Edition: All the copies of a book printed from a single setting of type—including all reprintings from standing type, from plates, or by photo-offset processes.

Printing: All the copies of an edition printed at one time (without removing the type or plates from the press).

Issue: Issues occur only within single printings and are created by an alteration affecting the conditions of publication or sale to *some* copies of a given printing. Issues occur in *The Man With the Golden Arm* and *Chicago: City on the Make.*

State: States occur only within single printings and are created by an alteration not affecting the conditions of publication in *some* copies of a given printing (by stop-press correction or cancellation of leaves). No states for Algren's books have been identified.

Edition, printing, issue, and *state* have been restricted to the sheets of the books. Binding and dust-jacket variants have no bearing on these terms. Nevertheless, the definition of *issue* incorporates the concept of marketing, so it is difficult to treat this term conservatively. In the present era of "quality paperbacks" or "trade paperbacks" a publisher may market the sheets of a printing simultaneously in cloth and wrappers—as with *The Devil's Stocking* (A 14.2.a). These binding variants do not create true *issues* because the sheets are not altered. (I have considered the term *binding issue* to accommodate these circumstances, but have reserved it for special cases—such as when the sheets are sold as "regular" and "limited" copies by virtue of a deluxe binding and numbering.) Remainder bindings present no such difficulties. Constable's "cheap edition" of *Somebody in Boots* (A 1.2) was an attempt to salvage unbound sheets without altering them; therefore it has been described as a binding variant. Dust jackets are frequently replaced or altered within a printing for marketing purposes—occasionally with a change of publisher. It is best to be cautious and treat variant dust jackets simply as variant dust jackets.

Issue and *state* are the most abused terms in the vocabulary of bibliographical description. Many cataloguers use them incorrectly and interchangeably. Much would be gained by the consistent and precise application of these terms.

Dust jackets for Section A entries have been described in detail because they are part of the original publication effort and sometimes provide information about how the book was marketed. There is, of course, no certainty that a jacket now on a copy of a book was originally on it.

For binding-cloth descriptions I have used the method proposed by G. Thomas Tanselle;[1] most of these cloth grains are illustrated in Jacob Blanck, ed., *The Bibliography of American Literature* (New Haven, Conn.: Yale University Press, 1955–   ).

Color specifications are taken from the *ISCC-NBS Color-Name Charts Illustrated with Centroid Colors* (National Bureau of Standards). In the descriptions of title pages, bindings, and dust jackets, the color of the lettering is always black, unless otherwise stipulated. The style of type is roman, unless otherwise stipulated. The spines of bindings and dust jackets are printed horizontally, unless otherwise stipulated.

The term *perfect binding* refers to books in which the pages are held together with adhesive along the back edge after the folds have been trimmed—for example, most paperbacks.

The locations rubric does not list every copy examined.

Dates provided within brackets do not appear on the title pages. Usually—but not invariably—they are taken from the copyright pages.

It is desirable in bibliographical descriptions to avoid end-of-line hyphens in

---

transcriptions. Because of word lengths and a measured line, however, it is impossible to satisfy this requirement in every case. End-of-line hyphens have been avoided wherever possible, and always where a hyphen would create ambiguity.

Locations are provided by the following symbols:

BL: British Library, London
LC: Library of Congress
Lilly: Lilly Library, Indiana University
MJB: Collection of Matthew J. Bruccoli
PSt: Pennsylvania State University Library
USC: Thomas Cooper Library, University of South Carolina

A bibliography is outdated the day it goes to the printer. Addenda and corrigenda are earnestly solicited.

The University of South Carolina
19 March 1985

A. Separate Publications

A 1 SOMEBODY IN BOOTS

A 1.1
First edition, only printing (1935)

Somebody
in Boots

A novel by Nelson Algren

The Vanguard Press · New York

A 1.1: 5½″ × 8⅛″

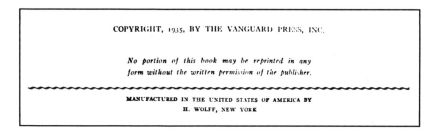

[i–x] [1–2] 3–90 [91–92] 93–188 [189–190] 191–291 [292–294] 295–322 [323–326]

[1–21]^8

Contents: pp. i–ii: blank; p. iii: half title; p. iv: blank; p. v: title; p. vi: copyright; p. vii: 'DEDICATED TO | THOSE INNUMERABLE THOUSANDS: | The Homeless Boys of America'; p. viii: blank; p. ix: acknowledgments and disclaimer; p. x: blank; p. 1: part title and epigraph from "Old Song"; p. 2: blank; pp. 3–90: text; p. 91: part title and epigraph from Baudelaire; p. 92: blank; pp. 93–188: text; p. 189: part title and epigraph from *The Communist Manifesto;* p. 190: blank; pp. 191–291: text; p. 292: blank; p. 293: part title and epigraph from *The Communist Manifesto;* p. 294: blank; pp. 295–322: text; pp. 323–326: blank. See C 3, C 4, C 5, C 8, C 10, C 13, C 14, C 18, C 72.

Typography and paper: 6⁵⁄₁₆″ (6½″) × 3¹³⁄₁₆″. 38 lines per page. No running heads. Wove paper.

Binding: Gray reddish orange (#39) V cloth (smooth). Spine stamped in black: '[thick rule] | [2 lines outlined against square] Somebody | in Boots | [thick rule] | ALGREN | [thick rule] | [thick rule] | VANGUARD | [thick rule]'. Front and bottom edges untrimmed. Top edge stained reddish brown. Off-white endpapers.

2nd binding: Light brown (#57) V cloth. Same stamping. Top edge not stained.

Dust jacket: Front: '[black, white, and bronze drawing of man's face with railroad yard in background, signed ENCK] [light green] SOMEBODY IN | BOOTS | NELSON ALGREN'. Spine: '[lettered in black against light green] SOMEBODY | IN BOOTS | NELSON | ALGREN | [reproduction of cover in white frame] | VANGUARD'. Back: ad for James T. Farrell's *Judgment Day.* Front flap has blurb for *Somebody in Boots.* Back flap has biographical note on Algren and order coupon.

Publication: Undetermined number of copies published 27 March 1935. $2.50. Copyright #A 81207.

Printing: Printed by A. S. Browne Printing Co., Hoboken, N.J.; bound by H. Wolff Estate, New York.

Locations: LC (MAR 28 1935), MJB, USC (dj), Lilly, Paul and Elizabeth Garon (second binding).

Dust jacket for A 1.1

A 1.2
First English edition, only printing (1935)

Somebody
in Boots

A novel by Nelson Algren

Constable & Co. Ltd. · London W.C.2

A 1.2: 4¾″ × 7¼″

```
┌─────────────────────────────────────────────────────────────────┐
│                         PUBLISHED BY                              │
│                   Constable and Company Ltd.                      │
│                            LONDON                                 │
│   ~~~~~~~~~~~~~~~~~~~~~~~~~~~~~~~~~~~~~~~~~~~~~~~~~~~~~~~~~~~~~~~    │
│                     First Published 1935                          │
│   ~~~~~~~~~~~~~~~~~~~~~~~~~~~~~~~~~~~~~~~~~~~~~~~~~~~~~~~~~~~~~~~    │
│     PRINTED IN GREAT BRITAIN BY THE WHITEFRIARS PRESS LTD.        │
│                  LONDON AND TONBRIDGE                             │
└─────────────────────────────────────────────────────────────────┘
```

[i–vi] vii [viii] [1–2] 3–112 [113–114] 115–221 [222–224] 225–347 [348–350] 351–382 [383–384]

[A] B–I K–U X–Z AA^8 BB^4

Contents: p. i: half title; p. ii: *'How Misery Lives'* [3 titles: *Waiting for Nothing* by Tom Kromer, *A Room in Berlin* by Günther Birkenfeld, *The Submerged Tenth* by John Bentley]; p. iii: title; p. iv: copyright; p. v: dedication; p. vi: 6-line disclaimer; p. vii: contents; p. viii: blank; p. 1: part title; p. 2: blank; pp. 3–112: text; p. 113: part title; p. 114: blank; pp. 115–221: text; p. 222: blank; p. 223: part title; p. 224: epigraph from *The Communist Manifesto;* pp. 225–347: text; p. 348: blank; p. 349: part title; p. 350: epigraph from *The Communist Manifesto;* pp. 351–382: text; pp. 383–384: blank.

Typography and paper: 5⅝″ (5¹³⁄₁₆″) × 3⅝⁄₁₆″. 34 lines per page. No running heads. Wove paper.

Binding: Blue-gray V cloth (smooth). Spine stamped in dark blue: 'Somebody | in Boots | [wavy rule] | nelson | algren | constable'. All edges trimmed. Top edge stained red. White endpapers.

Dust jacket: Not seen.

Publication: Undetermined number of copies published September 1935. 7/6.

Printing: See copyright page.

Location: BL (20 SEP 35).

First English edition, remainder binding ("cheap edition" of first-printing sheets).

Binding: Deep reddish orange (#36) V cloth (smooth); spine stamped in black: 'Somebody | in Boots | [wavy rule] | nelson | algren | [script] Constable'.

Dust jacket: Front and spine lettered in white against blue background. Front: 'SOMEBODY | IN BOOTS | [kneeling figure under hobnail boots] | NELSON | ALGREN'. Spine: 'SOMEBODY | IN BOOTS | NELSON | ALGREN | [three figures hopping freight] | [reddish orange] 2/6 | NET | [white] CONSTABLE'. Front flap has description of novel continued on back flap and back jacket with biographical note on Algren.

SOMEBODY IN BOOTS

NELSON ALGREN

SOMEBODY IN BOOTS

NELSON ALGREN

CONSTABLE

Dust jacket for A1.2

Publication: Undetermined number of copies distributed in 1937. 2/6.

Location: Lilly (dj).

A 1.3.a
Third edition, first printing: The Jungle. New York: Avon, [1957].

#T-185. Wrappers. 35¢. On front: "An Adaptation of 'Somebody in Boots.' "

A 1.3.b
Third edition, second printing: The Jungle. New York: Avon, [1959].

#T-324. Wrappers. 35¢. On front: "Original title: Somebody in Boots (Abridged)."

A 1.4
Fourth edition, only printing: [London]: Mayflower-Dell, [1964].

#8110. Wrappers. 4s.

A 1.5
Fifth edition, only printing: [New York]: Berkley Medallion, [1965].

#1125. Wrappers. 75¢. New "Preface" by Algren, pp. 5–9. See C 72.

A2 NEVER COME MORNING

A2.1.a
First edition, first printing (1942)

NEVER COME MORNING

by

NELSON ALGREN

WITH AN INTRODUCTION BY
RICHARD WRIGHT

Harper & Brothers Publishers

NEW YORK AND LONDON

A2.1.a: 5½″ × 8¹⁄₁₆″

NEVER COME MORNING
Copyright, 1941, 1942, by Nelson Algren
Printed in the United States of America
*All rights in this book are reserved. It may not be used for
dramatic, motion- or talking-picture purposes without
written authorization from the holder of these rights. Nor
may the book or part thereof be reproduced in any
manner whatsoever without permission in writing except
in the case of brief quotations embodied in critical articles and reviews. For information address: Harper &
Brothers, 49 East 33rd Street, New York, N. Y.*

4-2
FIRST EDITION
C-R

[i–viii] ix–x [xi–xvi] 1–284 [285–288]

[1–19]⁸

Contents: p. i: half title; p. ii: blank; p. iii: title; p. iv: copyright; p. v: *'For
Bernice'*; p. vi: blank; p. vii: contents; p. viii: blank; pp. ix–x: *'INTRODUCTION'*;
p. xi: acknowledgments and disclaimer; p. xii: blank; p. xiii: epigraph from
Whitman; p. xiv: blank; p. xv: half title; p. xvi: blank; pp. 1–284: text, headed
'BOOK I | *BELOW THE BELT* '; pp. 285–288: blank. See B 3, C 26.

Typography and paper: 6″ (6¼″) × 4⅛″. 36 lines per page. Running heads:
rectos, chapter titles; versos, 'NEVER COME MORNING'. Wove paper.

Binding: Dark blue (#183) V cloth (smooth). Spine goldstamped: '[thick rule,
thin rule, dotted rule] Never | Come | Morning | [circle] | NELSON | ALGREN |
[circle] | [Harper torch device] | *Harper* | [dotted rule, thin rule, thick rule]'. All
edges trimmed. Off-white endpapers.

Dust jacket: '[lettered in black against light green] [3-line blurb] | [following 4
lines against orange panel with city street scene] Never | Come | Morning |
[white] *a novel by* [black] *NELSON ALGREN* | [lettered in black against light
green] [5-line statement by Richard Wright] | [4-line statement by Harry
Hansen] | [white] *Harper and Brothers* | • | *Established 1817'*. Spine: '[con-
tinues background colors from front] *NELSON* | *ALGREN* | [white] Never |
Come | Morning | [black] *Harper'*. Back: photo of Algren by Reuben Segel with
biographical note. Front and back flaps have blurb for *Never Come Morning.*

Publication: Undetermined number of copies published 15 April 1942. $2.50.
Copyright #A 163237.

Printing: Produced by Haddon Craftsmen, Camden, N.J.

Locations: LC (rebound; received 8 APR 1942), MJB, USC (dj), Lilly (dj),
PSt.

NEVER COME MORNING

Never Come Morning

a novel by NELSON ALGREN

NELSON ALGREN
Never Come Morning

Harper

Harper and Brothers · Established 1817

Dust jacket for A.2.1.a

Note: Galleys bound in unprinted beige wrappers (Paul and Elizabeth Garon).

A 2.1.b
First edition, second printing: New York: Harper, [   ].

Not seen.

A 2.1.c
First edition, first English printing (1958)

NEVER COME MORNING

by

NELSON ALGREN

WITH AN INTRODUCTION BY
RICHARD WRIGHT

London
NEVILLE SPEARMAN

A 2.1.c: 5″ × 7¾″

'*Never Come Morning*'
was first published in 1958 *by*
Neville Spearman Limited
112 *Whitfield Street*
London W.1

© *All rights reserved*

It was printed in Great Britain by
D. R. Hillman & Sons Ltd.
Frome, Somerset

[i–vi] vii–viii [ix–x] 1–284 [285–286]

[A]⁴ B–I K¹⁶

Contents: p. i: half title; p. ii: card page [5 titles]; p. iii: title; p. iv: copyright; p. v: contents; p. vi: blank; pp. vii–viii: 'INTRODUCTION'; p. ix: 'For Jean-Paul Sartre'; p.x: epigraph from Whitman; pp. 1–284: text, headed: 'BOOK I | BELOW THE BELT'; pp. 285–286: blank.

Typography and paper: Same as first printing.

Binding: Dark blue (#183) paper-covered boards with V pattern (smooth). Spine goldstamped: 'Never | come | Morning | Nelson | algren | NEVILLE | SPEARMAN'. All edges trimmed. White endpapers.

Dust jacket: Front and spine lettered against deep red background. Front: '[black] BULITIS | [white] Never | Come | Morning | [black] nelson | algren | [drawing of woman and man] | [in deep red and white] By the author of "The Man with the Golden Arm" '. Spine: '[white] Never | come | Morning | [black] Nelson | algren | [drawing of man] | [black] NEVILLE | SPEARMAN'. Unprinted white back cover. Front flap has blurb. Back flap has ads for *The Ginger Man* by J. P. Donleavy, *A Walk on the Wild Side,* and *The Glass Playpen* by Edwina Mark.

Publication: Undetermined number of copies published August 1958. 15s.

Printing: See copyright page.

Locations: BL (27 AUG 58), MJB (dj).

A 2.1.d
First edition, second English printing: London: Neville Spearman, [   ].

Not seen.

A 2.1.e
First edition, fifth printing: New York, Evanston & London: Harper & Row, [1963].

Dust jacket for A2.1.c

Harper Colophon Books #CN15. Wrappers. $1.75. On front: 'complete and unabridged'. New preface by Algren, pp. ix–xiv. Dedicated to Candida Donadio.

A 2.2.a
Second edition, first printing: New York: Avon, [1948].

#185. Wrappers. 25¢. On front: 'SPECIALLY REVISED BY THE AUTHOR FOR AVON BOOKS'. Substantially rewritten.

A 2.2.e
Second edition, fifth printing: New York: Avon, [1952].

#419. Wrappers. 25¢. Copyright page lists Avon printings in November 1948, February 1949, April 1949, January 1950, and December 1951—totaling 950,000 copies.

A 2.2.g
Second edition, seventh printing: New York: Avon, [1955].

#T-108. Wrappers. 35¢. Copyright page: 'Seventh Avon Edition'.

A 2.2.h
Second edition, eighth printing: New York: Avon, [1958].

#T-223. Wrappers. 35¢.

A 2.3.a
Third edition, first printing: New York: Harper & Row, [1965].

Perennial Library #P4006B. Wrappers. 60¢.

A 2.3.b
Third edition, second printing: [New York]: Berkley, [1968].

Berkley Medallion Book #N1583. Wrappers. 95¢. On front: 'COMPLETE & UNEXPURGATED'. With Algren's preface.

A 2.4
Fourth edition, only printing: London: Corgi, [1964].

#FN1469. Wrappers. 5s.

A3 THE NEON WILDERNESS

A3.1.a
First edition, first printing (1947)

the

neon

wilderness

NELSON ALGREN

doubleday & co., inc., garden city, n.y. 1947

A3.1.a: 5⁵⁄₁₆″ × 7¹¹⁄₁₆″

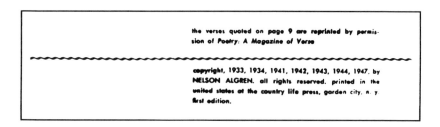

[1–17] 18–286 [287–288]. First page of each story unnumbered.

[1–9]^{16}

Contents: p. 1: half title; p. 2: card page; p. 3: title; p. 4: copyright; p. 5: 'for |
my mother | and the memory of | my father'; p. 6: blank; p. 7: disclaimer; p. 8:
blank; p. 9: epigraph from "The City" by David Wolff; p. 10: blank; p. 11:
acknowledgments; p. 12: blank; p. 13: contents; p. 14: blank; p. 15: half title;
p. 16: blank; pp. 17–286: text, headed: 'the captain has bad dreams *or who
put the sodium amytal in the hill & hill?*'; pp. 287–288: blank.

24 stories: "The Captain Has Bad Dreams,"* "How the Devil Came Down
Division Street" (B 6, C 35), "Is Your Name Joe?"* "Depend on Aunt Elly,"*
"Stickman's Laughter" (C 29), "A Bottle of Milk for Mother" (B 3, C 26), "He
Couldn't Boogie-Woogie Worth a Damn,"* "A Lot You Got to Holler,"* "Poor
Man's Pennies,"* "The Face on the Barroom Floor" (C 36), "The Brothers'
House" (B 1, C 11), "Please Don't Talk About Me When I'm Gone,"* "He
Swung and He Missed" (C 32), "El Presidente de Mejico,"* "Kingdom City to
Cairo,"* "That's the Way It's Always Been,"* "The Children" (C 34), "Million-
Dollar Brainstorm,"* "Pero Venceremos,"* "No Man's Laughter,"* "Katz,"*
"Design for Departure,"* "The Heroes,"* "So Help Me" (C 1). Asterisks indi-
cate previously unpublished stories.

Typography and paper: 5^{13}/₁₆″ (6¹/₁₆″) × 3^{13}/₁₆″. 35 lines per page. Wove
paper.

Binding: Light green (#144) V cloth (smooth). Spine lettered in dark yellow-
ish brown (#78): '[vertically] the neon wilderness • NELSON ALGREN | [hori-
zontally] doubleday'. Top edge stained dark yellowish brown. Top and bottom
edges trimmed. White endpapers.

Dust jacket: Front: '[white on green panel] A Collection of Short Stories | by
the Author of NEVER COME MORNING | [yellow on black panel] the | neon |
wilderness | [white on green panel] NELSON | ALGREN'. Spine: '[yellow on
green panel] NELSON | ALGREN | [yellow on black panel] the | neon | wilder- |
ness | [yellow on green panel] DOUBLEDAY'. Back has ads for *Idols of the
Cave* by Frederic Prokosch, *Asylum Piece* by Anna Kavan, *My Bird Sings* by
Oriel Malet, *Journey to the Interior* by P. H. Newby. Front flap: blurb for *The
Neon Wilderness*. Back flap: blurb for *My Past Was an Evil River* by George
Millar.

Dust jacket for A.3.1.a

Publication: 3,000 copies published 23 January 1947. $2.50. Copyright #A 10024.

Printing: See copyright page.

Locations: LC (received JAN 10 1947), MJB (dj), Lilly (dj).

A 3.1.b
First edition, second printing: Garden City: Doubleday, 1948.

1,000 copies.

A 3.1.c
First edition, third printing: Gloucester, Mass.: Peter Smith, 1968.

A 3.2.a
Second edition, first printing: New York: Avon, [1949].

#222. Wrappers. 25¢.

18 stories. Omits "A Bottle of Milk for Mother," "He Couldn't Boogie-Woogie Worth a Damn," "That's the Way It's Always Been," "Million-Dollar Brainstorm," "Katz," and "The Heroes."

A 3.2.b
Second edition, Canadian printing: New York: Avon, [1949].

Wrappers. Copyright page: 'PRINTED IN CANADA'.

A 3.2.c
Second edition, third printing: New York: Avon, [1952].

#424. Wrappers. 25¢.

A 3.2.d
Second edition, fourth printing: New York: Avon, [1956].

#T-125. Wrappers. 35¢.

A 3.3.a
Third edition, first printing: New York: Hill & Wang, 1960.

24 stories. American Century series. #AC27. Wrappers. $1.45. New introduction by Algren, pp. 9–14.

A 3.3.b
Third edition, second printing: New York: Hill & Wang, 1962.

#AC27. Wrappers. Dedication altered: 'for ruth reinhardt of jazz, ltd., chicago'.

A 3.3.c
Third edition, first English printing (1965)

the
neon
wilderness

NELSON ALGREN

 Andre Deutsch

A 3.3.c: 5" × 7¾"

first published 1965 by
ANDRE DEUTSCH LIMITED
105 Great Russell Street
London WC1
copyright, 1933, 1934, 1941, 1942, 1943,
1944, 1947, 1960 by NELSON ALGREN
all rights reserved
printed in Great Britain by
D. R. HILLMAN & SONS LTD
Frome, Somerset

all names appearing in this volume are fictitious; no
character or situation depicted is drawn from life. If
any name used happens to be that of an actual person,
it is a coincidence of which the author has no present
knowledge.

acknowledgment is made to the following magazines
for permission to reprint the stories indicated: To
American Mercury for "He Swung and He Missed" and
"The Children"; to *Story* for "So Help Me" and "The
Brothers' House"; to *Southern Review* for "Stickman's
Laughter" and "A Bottle of Milk for Mother"; and to
Harper's Bazaar for "How the Devil Came Down Division
Street."

the verses quoted on page 6 are reprinted by permission of *Poetry: A Magazine of Verse.*

[1–9] 10–14 [15–17] 18–286 [287–288]. First page of each story unnumbered.

[A] B–I[16]

Contents: p. 1: blurb; p. 2: card page [6 titles]; p. 3: title; p. 4: copyright; p. 5:
'for | ruth reinhardt | of | jazz, ltd., chicago'; p. 6: epigraph from "The City" by
David Wolff; p. 7: contents; p. 8: blank; pp. 9–14: 'introduction'; p. 15: half title;
p. 16: blank; pp. 17–286: text, headed: 'the captain has bad dreams | or who
put the sodium amytal in the hill & hill?'; pp. 287–288: blank. 24 stories.

Typography and paper: 5$\frac{13}{16}$" (6$\frac{1}{16}$") × 3$\frac{13}{16}$". 35 lines per page. Running
heads: rectos, story titles; versos, 'the neon wilderness'. Wove paper.

Binding: Strong red (#12) paper-covered boards. Spine goldstamped: 'The |
Neon | Wilderness | [two rules] | NELSON | ALGREN | [bow-and-arrows de-
vice] | André Deutsch'. All edges trimmed. White endpapers.

Dust jacket: Front: '[light blue] THE | [in white dots on strong purplish red
lettering] Neon | [white] WILDERNESS | [reddish purple lettering on light blue
panel] NELSON ALGREN | [preceding 4 lines surrounded by strong purplish
red dots] | [line of white dots] | [black drawing of men against reddish purple]'.

Dust jacket for A.3.3.c

Spine: '[against reddish purple: two lines of strong purplish red dots] | [white] THE | NEON | WILDER- | NESS | [two lines of strong purplish red dots] | [white] NELSON | ALGREN | [black] [bow-and-arrows device] | ANDRE | DEUTSCH'. Back: list of 21 Deutsch titles. Front flap: blurb for *The Neon Wilderness*. Back flap: photo of Nelson Algren by Stephen Deutch and biographical note.

Publication: Undetermined number of copies published January 1965. 21s.

Printing: See copyright page.

Locations: BL (12 JAN 65), MJB (dj), Lilly (dj).

A 3.3.d
Third edition, fourth printing: New York: Hill & Wang, [1966].

#AC27. Wrappers. Copyright page: 'Third Printing December 1966'.

A 3.3.e
Third edition, fifth printing: New York: Hill & Wang, 1975.

#AC27. Wrappers.

A 3.4
Fourth edition, only printing: [New York]: Berkley Medallion, [1965].

24 stories. #S1103. Wrappers. 75¢.

A 3.5
Fifth edition: [London]: Mayflower, [1968].

#6296-8. Wrappers. 5s.

A 4 THE MAN WITH THE GOLDEN ARM

A 4.1.a₁
First edition, first printing, trade issue (1949)

THE MAN

WITH

a novel by Nelson Algren

THE GOLDEN

ARM

doubleday & company, inc., garden city, n.y., 1949

A 4.1.a: 5⁹⁄₁₆″ × 8⅛″

[i–viii] [1–2] 3–200 [201–202] 203–343 [344]

[1–11]¹⁶

Contents: p. i: half title; p. ii: card page [4 titles]; p. iii: title; p. iv: copyright; p. v: '*For Amanda*'; p. vi: acknowledgment to Newberry Library; p. vii: contents; p. viii: blank; p. 1: part title; p. 2: epigraph from Kuprin; pp. 3–200: text; p. 201: part title; p. 202: epigraph from Fitzgerald; pp. 203–342: text; p. 343: 'EPITAPH: The Man with the Golden Arm'; p. 344: blank. See A 13, C 38, C 41.

Typography and paper: 6⁹⁄₁₆″ (6¾″) × 4⁵⁄₁₆″. 38 lines per page. No running heads. Wove paper.

Binding: Yellow-gray (#93) V cloth (smooth). Spine stamped in very red (#11) and very dark green (#147): '[very red] THE MAN | [very dark green]

Dust jacket for A4.1.a

WITH | [very red] THE GOLDEN | [very dark green] ARM | [very dark green spade] | [very dark green] BY | [very red] NELSON ALGREN | [very dark green rule] | DOUBLEDAY'. Top edge stained gray-olive. Fore-edge untrimmed. Bottom edge rough-trimmed. Very dark green (#147) coated endpapers.

Dust jacket: White background. Front: '[medium yellow-green] A NOVEL | BY THE AUTHOR OF 'NEVER COME MORNING' | [black] NELSON ALGREN | [very red and black] tHe | [black drawing of hypodermic needle] | [black] MaN | [medium yellow-green, very red, and black] WItH tHe | GOLDeN | ARM | [black spade] | [medium yellow-green] KAROV'. Spine: '[medium yellow-green] tHe | MaN | WitH tHe | GOLDeN | ARM | [black spade] | [very red] NeLSON | ALGReN | [medium yellow-green] DOUBLEDAY'. Back has photo of Algren by Robert McCullough and blurbs. Front and back flaps have blurb and list of characters.

Publication: 10,000 copies published 8 August 1949. $3.00. Copyright #A 35815.

Printing: See copyright page.

Locations: LC (received SEP 12 1949), MJB (dj), USC (dj), Lilly (dj).

A 4.1.a₂
First edition, first printing, signed issue

[i–x] [1–2] 3–200 [201–202] 203–343 [344]

$[1]^{16}$ $(1+1_1)$ $[2–11]^{16}$

Unprinted leaf signed by Algren on recto tipped in at front. Undetermined number of copies. Location: USC (dj).

Note: Advance proofs bound in wrappers. Not seen.

A 4.1.b
First edition, second printing: New York: Doubleday, 1949.

2,500 copies. September 1949.

Note: The information that there were eight printings of the first edition is based on the Doubleday records.
  Four Doubleday printings dated 1949 on title pages can be differentiated: (a) First printing identified as 'FIRST EDITION' on copyright page. (b) First edition designation removed. (c) Acknowledgment for *Yama* added to second paragraph on copyright page. (d) Haddon Craftsmen printer's imprint substituted for Country Life Press on copyright page. Possibly a book club printing.
  Progressive folio batter has been noted on pp. 7, 97, 262, 277, 320, 328.

A 4.1.c
First edition, third printing: New York: Doubleday, 1949.

7,500 copies. December 1949.

A sampling of paperback wrappers

A 4.1.d
First edition, fourth printing: New York, Doubleday, 1950.

3,500 copies. March 1950.

A 4.1.e
First edition, fifth printing: New York: Doubleday, 1950.

2,500 copies. March 1950. One copy with 1950 title page seen. Printing sequence undetermined.

A 4.1.f
First edition, sixth printing: New York: Doubleday, [   ].

5,000 copies.

A 4.1.g
First edition, seventh printing: New York: Doubleday, 1955.

1,000 copies.

A 4.1.h
First edition, eighth printing: New York: Doubleday, [1956].

1,000 copies. May 1956.

Note 1: *The Man with the Golden Arm* was the Book Find Club selection for January 1950.

Note 2: Condensed in *Book Digest,* 1 (April 1950), 3–43.

Note 3: A dramatic version by Jack Kirkland opened at the Cherry Lane Theatre, New York, 21 May 1956.

A 4.1.i
First edition, first English printing (1959)
[i–vi] [1–2] 3–200 [201–202] 203–343 [344–346]

[1–11]^{16}

Contents: p. i–ii: pastedown endpaper; p. iii: half title; p. iv: card page [5 titles]; p. v: title; p. vi: copyright; p. 1: dedication and contents; p. 2: epigraph from Kuprin; pp. 3–200: text; p. 201: part title; p. 202: epigraph from Fitzgerald; pp. 203–342: text; p. 343: 'EPITAPH: The Man with the Golden Arm'; p. 344: blank; pp. 345–346: rear pastedown endpaper.

Typography and paper: Same as first printing.

Binding: Black paper-covered boards with V pattern (smooth). Spine gold-stamped: 'the | man | with | the | golden | arm | nelson | algren | Neville | Spearman'. All edges trimmed.

Dust jacket: Front and spine lettered against black background. Front: '[white] the man with | the golden arm | [on 5 white panels: very red arm and hand holding cards; hypodermic needle] | [white] FORT | nelson algren'. Spine: '[very red] nelson | algren | [vertically in white] the man with the golden arm | [horizontally in very red] NEVILLE | SPEARMAN'. Back has blurbs for *A Walk on the Wild Side* and *Never Come Morning*. Front flap has blurb for *The Man with the Golden Arm;* back flap has blurbs for *The Ginger Man* by J. P. Donleavy and *Elisa* by Edmond de Goncourt.

Publication: Undetermined number of copies published February 1959. 16s.

Printing: See copyright page.

Locations: BL (9 FEB 59), MJB (dj), Lilly (dj).

4.1.j
First edition, tenth printing: Cambridge, Mass.: Robert Bentley, [1978].

"With an Appreciation of Nelson Algren by Studs Terkel."

THE MAN

WITH

a novel by Nelson Algren

THE GOLDEN

ARM

Neville Spearman, London

A 4.1.j: 5³⁄₁₆″ × 7¹¹⁄₁₆″

'The Man with the Golden Arm'
was first published in 1959 by
Neville Spearman Limited
112 Whitfield Street
London W.1
© *All rights reserved*
It was made and printed in Great Britain by
A. Wheaton & Company Limited, Exeter

A 4.2.a
Second edition, first printing: New York: Pocket Books, [1951].

#757. Wrappers. 25¢. Copyright page: '1st printing . . . January, 1951'. Re-released December 1951 in dust jacket as Cardinal C-31; 35¢ (Kenneth G. McCollum).

A 4.2.b
Second edition, second printing: New York: Pocket Books, [1956].

Cardinal #C-31. Wrappers. 35¢. Copyright page: '2nd printing . . . January, 1956'.

A 4.2.c
Second edition, third printing: New York: Pocket Books, [1956].

Cardinal #C-31. Wrappers. 35¢. Copyright page: '3rd printing . . . January, 1956'.

A 4.2.d
Second edition, fourth printing: New York: Pocket Books, [1956].

Cardinal #C-31. Wrappers. 35¢. Copyright page: '4th printing . . . February, 1956'.

A 4.2.e
Second edition, fifth printing: New York: Pocket Books, [1956].

Cardinal #C-31. Wrappers. 35¢. Copyright page: '5th printing . . . February, 1956'.

A 4.2.f
Second edition, sixth printing: New York: Pocket Books, [1956].

Cardinal #C-31. Wrappers. 35¢. Copyright page: '6th printing . . . April, 1956'.

A 4.2.g
Second edition, seventh printing: New York: Pocket Books, [1956].

Cardinal #C-31. Wrappers. 35¢. Copyright page: '7th printing . . . June, 1956'.

Dust jacket for A4.1.j

A 4.3
Third edition, only printing: London: Ace, [1961].

#H414. Wrappers. 3/6.

A 4.4
Fourth edition, only printing: London: Transworld, [1964].

Corgi #FN1468. Wrappers. 5s.

A 4.5.a
Fifth edition, first printing: Greenwich, Conn.: Fawcett Crest, [1964].

#t727. Copyright page: 'First Crest printing, June 1964'. Wrappers. 75¢.

A 4.5.b
Fifth edition, Canadian printing: Greenwich, Conn.: Fawcett Crest, [1964].

#t727. Copyright page: 'Printed in Canada'. Wrappers. 75¢.

A 4.5.c
Fifth edition, third printing: Greenwich, Conn.: Fawcett Premier, [1970].

#M511. Copyright page: 'June 1964 | November 1970'. Wrappers. 95¢.

A 4.5.d
Fifth edition, fourth printing: Greenwich, Conn.: Fawcett Crest, [   ].

#m956. Wrappers. 95¢.

A 4.5.e
Fifth edition, fifth printing: Greenwich, Conn.: Fawcett Crest, [   ].

#M1189. Wrappers. 95¢.

A 4.6
Sixth edition, only printing: Portway, Bath: Cedric Chivers, [1973].

Copyright page: 'This edition published by Cedric Chivers Ltd by arrangement with the copyright holder at the request of The London & Home Counties Branch of The Library Association 1972'.

A 4.7.a
Seventh edition, first printing: [New York]: Penguin, [1977].

Wrappers. $2.50. Copyright page: 'Published in Penguin Books . . . 1977'.

A 4.8.a
Eighth edition, first printing: [New York]: Penguin, [1984].

Wrappers. $5.95.

A 5 CHICAGO: CITY ON THE MAKE

A 5.1.a
First edition, first printing (1951)

A 5.1.a: 8¾″ × 7¼″

[i–ii] [1–13] 14–22 [23] 24–35 [36–37] 38–50 [51] 52–60 [61] 62–72 [73] 74–83 [84–85] 86–92 [93–94]

$[1-6]^8$

Contents: p. i–ii: blank; p. 1: half title; p. 2: blank; p. 3: card page [5 titles]; pp. 4–5: title; p. 6: copyright; p. 7: 'FOR | CARL | SANDBURG'; p. 8: blank; p. 9: epigraph from Baudelaire; p. 10: blank; p. 11: contents; p. 12: blank; p. 13: *'one'*; pp. 14–22: text; p. 23: *'two'*; pp. 24–35: text; p. 36: blank; p. 37: *'three'*; pp. 38–50: text; p. 51: *'four'*; pp. 52–60: text; p. 61: *'five'*; pp. 62–72: text; p. 73: *'six'*; pp. 74–83: text; p. 84: blank; p. 85: *'seven'*; pp. 86–92: text; pp. 93–94: blank.

Typography and paper: 5¼" (5⅝") × 3⅛". 27 lines per page. Running heads, versos only: chapter titles. Wove paper.

Binding: Medium gray (#265) paper-covered boards. Black cloth spine silver-stamped vertically: *'chicago: city on the make • Nelson Algren* DOUBLEDAY'. Top edge stained dark gray. All edges trimmed. White endpapers.

Dust jacket: Front: dark gray-green and medium purplish red panels with photo of Chicago: '[white] CHICAGO: | CITY | ON | THE | MAKE | [black script] by | [white script] Nelson Algren | [black] AUTHOR OF | [white] THE MAN WITH | THE GOLDEN ARM'. Spine: '[vertically] [white on dark gray-green] CHICAGO: CITY ON THE MAKE NELSON ALGREN DOUBLEDAY'. Back has photos of Chicago and Algren by Robert McCullough, with excerpt from text. Front flap has blurb; rear flap has note on Algren and blurbs.

Publication: 5,000 copies published 18 October 1951. $1.50. Copyright #A60168.

Printing: See copyright page.

Locations: MJB (dj), Lilly (dj).

Note: A version of *Chicago: City on the Make* appeared as "One Man's Chicago," *Holiday*, 10 (October 1951). See C 51, C 219.

A 5.1.b
First edition, second printing: New York: Doubleday, 1951.

5,000 copies.

Dust jacket for A.5.1.a

A 5.2.a
Second edition, first printing (augmented): Sausalito, Cal.: Contact Editions, 1961.

#R1. Wrappers. 95¢. Adds introduction, "The People Of These Parts: A Survey of Modern Mid-American Letters," pp. 8–35. Dedication altered: *'For Herman and Marilou Kogan'*.

A 5.2.b₁
Second edition, second printing, first issue: Oakland, Cal.: Angel Island, [1968].

Copyright page: *'Third Edition'*. Wrappers. $2.45. 100 copies supplied to Algren with new epilogue titled "Ode to Kissassville or: Gone on the Arfy-Darfy." Dedication altered: 'FOR JOAN BAEZ | *A conscience in touch with humanity'*. Location: Kenneth McCollum. See C 138.

A 5.2.b₂
Second edition, second printing, second issue: Oakland, Cal.: Angel Island, [1968].

Wrappers. $2.45. Copyright page: *'Third Edition'*. Epilogue titled "Ode to Lower Finksville."

A 5.3.a
Third edition, first printing: New York: McGraw-Hill, [1983].

Copyright page: 'First McGraw-Hill Paperback edition, 1983'. Wrappers. $5.95. Introduction by Studs Terkel. Omits epilogue and moves Algren's introduction to afterword. Dedicated to Algren.

A 6 A WALK ON THE WILD SIDE

A 6.1.a
First edition, first printing (1956)

Nelson Algren

A WALK
ON THE
WILD
SIDE

Farrar, Straus and Cudahy
NEW YORK

A 6.1.a: 5½″ × 8⅛″

© 1956 by Nelson Algren
Library of Congress catalog card number 56-8623
First printing, 1956

The lines from "Chinatown" are reprinted by permission of the copyright owner, Remick Music Corporation. The lines from "I Didn't Raise My Boy To Be A Soldier," words by Alfred Bryan, music by Al Piantadosi, are copyright 1915/copyright renewal 1943 by Leo Feist, Inc. Used by permission. The lines from "Why Don't You Do Right" are reprinted by permission of the copyright owner, Mayfair Music Corp. The lines from "All Of Me," published 1931 by Bourne, Inc., are reprinted by permission of the copyright owner.

Published simultaneously in Canada by Ambassador Books, Ltd.
Manufactured in the U. S. A.
American Book-Stratford Press, Inc., New York

[i–vi] [1–2] 3–114 [115–116] 117–284 [285–286] 287–346

[1–11]^{16}

Contents: p. i: half title; p. ii: card page [6 titles]; p. iii: title; p. iv: copyright; p. v: 'To | Elizabeth Ingersoll'; p. vi: blank; p. 1: 'ONE'; p. 2: blank; pp. 3–114: text; p. 115: 'TWO'; p. 116: blank; pp. 117–284: text; p. 285: 'THREE'; p. 286: blank; pp. 287–346: text. See B 13, B 15, C 8, C 36, C 63, C 64.

Typography and paper: 6³⁄₁₆" (6⅝") × 4". 35 lines per page. Running heads: across verso and recto: *'A WALK ON THE WILD SIDE'*. Wove paper.

Binding: Gray-blue (#186) paper-covered boards front and back. Front embossed: '[vertically up in black script] Nelson Algren | [horizontally in light olive-brown (#94)] A WALK | ON THE | WILD | SIDE'. Brilliant orange-yellow (#67) paper-covered spine: '[vertically up in black] *NELSON ALGREN* | [medium gray (#265) horizontal rule] | [horizontally in medium gray] A WALK | ON THE | WILD | SIDE | [horizontal medium gray rule] | [vertically up in black] *FARRAR, STRAUS AND CUDAHY'*. All edges trimmed. White endpapers. Noted with and without top edge stained reddish brown.

Dust jacket: Front has photo of Algren in alley with tilted lettering: '[yellow] A | WALK | ON THE | WILD SIDE | [white] by NELSON ALGREN | author of THE MAN WITH THE GOLDEN ARM'. Spine lettered on black background: '[yellow] A | WALK | ON THE | WILD | SIDE | [white] NELSON | ALGREN | FARRAR | STRAUS | AND | CUDAHY'. Back has biographical note and statement by Algren. Front and back flaps have blurb, including statement by Algren.

Publication: Undetermined number of copies published 21 May 1956. $4.50. Copyright #A239631.

Printing: Produced by American Book—Stratford Press, New York.

Locations: LC (rebound; JUN-7 1956), MJB (dj; top edge unstained), Lilly (dj; top edge stained), Paul and Elizabeth Garon (with and without top edge stained), USC (top edge unstained).

A WALK
ON THE
WILD
SIDE

NELSON
ALGREN

FARRAR
STRAUS
AND
CUDAHY

by NELSON ALGREN

author of THE MAN WITH THE GOLDEN ARM

NELSON ALGREN
*Winner of the first
NATIONAL BOOK AWARD*

*A Walk on the
Wild Side*

continued on back flap

FARRAR, STRAUS AND CUDAHY
101 Fifth Avenue, New York 3, N.Y.

Dust jacket for A.6.1.a

A 6.1.b
First edition, second printing: New York: Farrar, Straus & Cudahy, [1956].

On dust jacket flap: 'Second large printing'.

A 6.1.c
First edition, later printing: New York: Farrar, Straus & Cudahy, [   ].

A 6.1.d
First edition, first English printing (1957)

Nelson Algren

A WALK
ON THE
WILD
SIDE

Neville Spearman
LONDON

A 6.1.d: 5″ × 7^{11}⁄₁₆″

> *'A Walk on the Wild Side'*
> *was first published in* 1957 *by*
> *Neville Spearman Limited*
> 112 *Whitfield Street*
> *London W.*1
>
> *All rights reserved*
>
> *It was printed in Great Britain by*
> *D. R. Hillman & Sons Ltd.*
> *Frome, Somerset*

Same pagination as first Farrar, Straus and Cudahy printing.

[A] B–I K–L^{16}

Contents: Same as first Farrar, Straus and Cudahy printing.

Typography and paper: Same as first Farrar, Straus and Cudahy printing.

Binding: Deep red-orange (#36) paper-covered boards with V pattern (smooth). Spine goldstamped: 'Algren | A | WALK | ON | THE | WILD | SIDE | NEVILLE | SPEARMAN'. All edges trimmed. White endpapers.

Dust jacket: Front and spine have black and white movie still from *A Streetcar Named Desire*. Front: '[black on three yellow bands] A WALK ON THE | WILD SIDE | NELSON ALGREN | [yellow] the author of | The Man with the Golden Arm'. Spine: '[vertically in yellow] Algren A WALK ON THE WILD SIDE Spearman'. Unprinted white back cover. Front flap reprints Farrar, Straus and Cudahy blurb with Algren statement. Back flap has excerpts from reviews for *A Walk on the Wild Side* and *The Ginger Man* by J. P. Donleavy.

Publication: Undetermined number of copies published July 1957. 15s.

Printing: See copyright page.

Locations: BL (18 JUL 1957), MJB (dj).

A 6.1.e
First edition, second English printing: London: Neville Spearman, [   ].

Not seen.

A 6.1.f
First edition, third English printing: London: Neville Spearman, [   ].

Not seen.

A 6.1.g
First edition, seventh printing: Westport, Conn.: Greenwood Press, [1978].

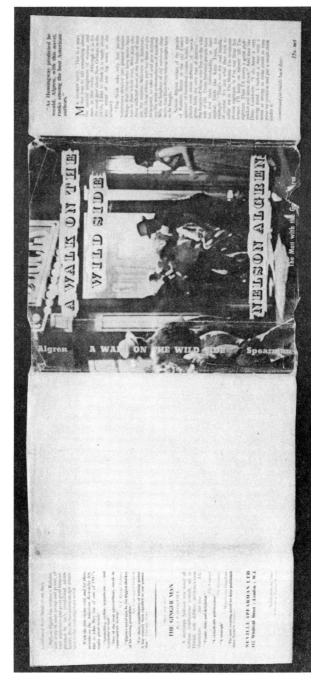

Dust jacket for A6.1.d

A6.2.a
Second edition, first printing: Greenwich, Conn.: Fawcett, [1957].

Crest Giant #d157. Copyright page: 'First CREST printing, January 1957'. Wrappers. 50¢. Minor revisions by Algren.

A6.2.b
Second edition, second printing: Greenwich, Conn.: Fawcett, [1957].

Crest Giant #d157. Copyright page: 'Second CREST printing, May 1957'. Wrappers. 50¢.

A6.2.c
Second edition, third printing: Greenwich, Conn.: Fawcett, [1960].

Crest Giant #d377. Copyright page: 'Third CREST printing May 1960'. Wrappers. 50¢.

A6.3.a
Third edition, first printing: Greenwich, Conn.: Fawcett, [1962].

Crest #d496. Copyright page: 'Fourth Crest printing, January 1962'. Wrappers. 50¢.

A6.3.b
Third edition, Canadian printing: Greenwich, Conn.: Fawcett, [1962].

Crest #d496. Copyright page: 'Second Crest printing, February 1962. . . . Printed in Canada'. Wrappers. 50¢. Presumably the second Canadian printing; first printing not seen.

A6.3.c
Third edition, third printing: Greenwich, Conn.: Fawcett, [1962].

Crest #d496. Copyright page: 'Fifth Crest printing, April 1962'. Wrappers. 50¢.

A6.3.d
Third edition, fourth printing: Greenwich, Conn.: Fawcett, [1962].

Crest #d496. Copyright page: 'Sixth Crest printing, September 1962'. Wrappers. 50¢.

A6.3.e
Third edition, fifth printing: Greenwich, Conn.: Fawcett, [1963].

Crest #d496. Copyright page: 'SEVENTH CREST PRINTING, MARCH 1963'. Wrappers. 50¢.

A6.3.f
Third edition, unidentified printing: Greenwich, Conn.: Fawcett Crest, [   ].

#t890. Wrappers. 75¢.

A 6.3.g
Third edition, unidentified printing: Greenwich, Conn.: Fawcett Crest, [   ].

#M1238. Wrappers. 95¢.

A 6.4.a
Fourth edition, first printing: London: Transworld, [1964].

Corgi #FN1467. Wrappers. 5s.

A 6.5.a
Fifth edition, first printing: Portway, Bath: Cedric Chivers, [1973].

Copyright page: 'This edition published by Cedric Chivers Ltd by arrangement with the copyright holder at the request of The London & Home Counties Branch of The Library Association 1973'.

A 6.6.a
Sixth edition, first printing: [New York]: Penguin, [1977].

Copyright page: 'Published in Penguin Books 1977'. Wrappers. $2.50.

A 6.7.a
Seventh edition, first printing: [New York]: Penguin, [1984].

Wrappers. $5.95.

A 7 PROGRAM FOR A WALK ON THE WILD SIDE MUSICAL

A 7.1
Only edition, only printing (1960)

CAST

DOVE	Robert Dorough
TERESINA	Kelley Stephens
FINNERTY	James Inman
SCHMIDT	Joseph Cusanelli
HALLIE	Gladys Rankin
FLORALEE	Jan Goldin
FRENCHY	Marla Stevens
REBA	Jan Cagle
MAMA	Penny Hodges
DOC	William Powers

Chorus of   John Kelso
Characters   William Powers
             Dick Gibson
             Ralph Lowenstein

ORCHESTRA

Jimmy Williams	Piano
Billy Schneider	Drums
Terry Keppenberger	Bass

MUSICAL NUMBERS

ACT ONE

Scene One: Evening, Hobo Jungle
1. The Evenin' Weeries .... Dove
2. Fine Ol' Summer of '31 .... Dove & Chorus

Scene Two: Late Afternoon, Chili Parlor, Rio Grande Valley
3. No Warm Ups, No Wee Bits .... Teresina
4. Specialty Speckledy Gravy .... Dove
5. Teresina's Song .... Teresina

Scene Three: Next Morning
6. World Shaker .... Dove
7. Reprise: Teresina's Song .... Teresina

ACT TWO

Scene One: 1 Month Later, Perdido Street, New Orleans
The House of the Hundred Grass Fires
1. The House of the Hundred Grass Fires .... Chorus
2. What I Got? .... Dove
3. Finnerty's Song .... Finnerty

Scene Two: Afternoon, 2 Months Later
4. Reprise: World Shaker .... Dove
5. My Heart Will Always Be Your Home .... Hallie and Schmidt
6. Oh, Lovely Appearance of Death* .... Floralee
7. The Man on Wheels .... Schmidt

ACT THREE

Scene One: That Evening, Spare Nobody Bar
1. The Spare Nobody Bar .... Finnerty, Doc & Chorus
2. Your Name In Secret I Would Write* .... Dove
3. This Life We've Led .... Hallie
4. Alamo (Song For a Mexican Mistress) .... Dove and Teresina
*Lyrics based on old Folk Song.

The **CRYSTAL PALACE** Theatre
PRESENTS
The World Premiere of a new —
MUSICAL

Based on the novel by
NELSON ALGREN

Produced by
JAY LANDESMAN AND DAVID PELTZ

Book by
NELSON ALGREN   JAY LANDESMAN

Music by
TOMMY WOLF

Lyrics by
NELSON ALGREN   FRAN LANDESMAN

Directed by
DAVID PELTZ

DAVE MOON   DICK GIBSON   JULIETTE REED
Sets   Lighting   Costumes

Choreographed by
JAN GOLDIN

Introducing
ROBERT DOROUGH

Featuring
JOSEPH CUSANELLI,   KELLEY STEPHENS,
JAMES INMAN,   GLADYS RANKIN,
Jan Goldin, William Powers and Marla Stevens
with
John Kelso, Dick Gibson, Jan Cagle, Penny Hodges
and Ralph Lowenstein
Master Electrician: Walter Brechenkamp

Program for A 7.1

[1–8]

[1]⁴ Single sheet folded twice.

Contents: recto: cover, cast, musical numbers, credits; verso: 10 lyrics by Algren and Fran Landesman—"The Evenin' Wearies," "Teresina's Song," "Worldshaker," "My Heart Will Always Be Your Home," "The Fine Ol' Summer of '31," "This Life We've Led," "No Warm Ups, No Wee Bits," "The Man on Wheels," "The Spare Nobody Bar," "Alamo (Song for a Mexican Mistress)."

Paper: Orange wove paper printed in black.

Publication: Undetermined number of copies distributed at performances, the Crystal Palace, St. Louis, Missouri, commencing 11 February 1960. Show book coauthored by Algren and Jay Landesman; produced by Landesman and David Peltz.

Location: Jay Landesman.

SHEET MUSIC FOR MUSICAL
Performance sheet music reproduced from manuscript by photostat process. Music by Tommy Wolf; lyrics by Fran Landesman and Algren. Los Angeles: Wolf-Mills Music, Inc.

"The Fine Ol' Summer of '31" (© 1962), "The Evenin' Wearies" (© 1960), "Finnerty's Song," "The House of the Hundred Grassfires" (© 1962), "The Man on Wheels" (© 1962), "My Heart Will Always Be Your Home" (© 1963), "No Warm Ups—No Wee Bits," "Oh, Lovely Appearance of Death" (© 1960)—based on a song by George Whitefield, "Song for a Mexican Mistress (Remember the Alamo)," "The Spare Nobody Bar" (© 1962), "Specially Speckledy Gravy" (© 1961), "The Moon Is Feeling Wild Tonight (Teresina's Song)" (© 1961), "This Life We've Led" (© 1960), "What I Got?" (© 1960), "World Shaker" (© 1961), "Your Name in Secret I Would Write."

Location: MJB.

A 8 NELSON ALGREN'S OWN BOOK OF LONESOME MONSTERS

A 8.1.a
First edition, first printing (1962)

NELSON ALGREN'S
OWN BOOK OF
LONESOME
MONSTERS

LANCER BOOKS, INC. • 26 WEST 47TH STREET • NEW YORK 36, N.Y.

A 8.1.a: 4¼" × 7⅛"

A LANCER BOOK • 1962

FOR CANDIDA,

not an agent—a possession

THE HOUSE OF A HUNDRED GRASSFIRES from A WALK ON THE
WILD SIDE
ⓒ 1956 by Nelson Algren, F.S&C
PEACETIME by Brock Brower, NWW #19
ⓒ 1961 by J. B. Lippincott Co.
A WORLD FULL OF GREAT CITIES by Joseph Heller
ⓒ 1955 by Manvis Publications, Inc.
CLOSING OF THIS DOOR by Chandler Brossard, The Dial —1962
ⓒ 1962 by the Dial Press, Inc.
THE SHORES OF SCHIZOPHRENIA by Hughes Rudd
ⓒ by J. B. Lippincott Company 1961
HUNDRED DOLLAR EYES by Bernard Farbar
ⓒ 1962 by Bernard Farbar
THE MAN WHO KNEW WHAT ETHIOPIA SHOULD DO ABOUT HER
WATER TABLE by H. E. F. Donohue
ⓒ 1961 by Carleton College, Carleton Miscellany
SHOW BIZ CONNECTIONS by Bruce Jay Friedman
ⓒ 1962 by Bruce Jay Friedman
AMONG THE DANGS by George P. Elliott
ⓒ 1958 by George P. Elliott
ENTROPY by Thomas Pynchon, Kenyon Review
ⓒ 1960 by Thomas Pynchon
ADDRESS BY GOLEY MacDOWELL BEFORE THE HASBEENS CLUB
OF CHICAGO by Saul Bellow, Hudson Review
ⓒ 1961 by the Hudson Review
DAY OF THE ALLIGATOR by James Blake
ⓒ Paris Review #17 (1957)
TALK TO ME, TALK TO ME by Joan Kerckhoff
ⓒ 1962 by Joan Kerckhoff

All rights reserved.
Printed in the U.S.A.

LANCER BOOKS, INC. • 26 WEST 47TH STREET • NEW YORK 36, N.Y.

[1–6] 7–192.

Perfect binding.

Contents: p. 1: blurb; p. 2: Lancer ad; p. 3: title; p. 4: copyright and dedication: 'FOR CANDIDA, not an agent—a possession'; p. 5: contents; p. 6: blank; pp. 7–10: "The Book of Lonesome Monsters A Preface"; pp. 11–192: text.

13 stories: "World Full of Great Cities" by Joseph Heller, "Talk to Me, Talk to Me" by Joan Kerckhoff, "Show Biz Connections" by Bruce J. Friedman, "Hundred Dollar Eyes" by Bernard Farbar, "The Man Who Knew What Ethiopia Should Do about Her Water-Table" by H.E.F. Donohue, "Among the

Back wrapper for A8.1.a

Only NELSON ALGREN, author of Man With The Golden Arm and A Walk On The Wild Side, could have put together this book!

Gathered in this extraordinary collection are exciting stories by the most talented writers of our time.

Joseph Heller -author of **Catch-22**, literary sensation of the year.

Saul Bellow- **The Adventures of Augie March**, one of the most influential books of the last 50 years.

Chandler Brossard- author of the unforgettable "underground" novel," **The Bold Saboteurs.**

Brock Brower- **Esquire**'s leading (and most prolific) writer of fiction and non-fiction.

Thomas Pynchon- winner of the most important short story awards.

And the others. Nelson Algren's own discoveries. Writers, not of promise, but of accomplishment.

LANDER ORIGINAL 73-409 60¢

Nelson Algren's
OWN BOOK OF
LONESOME MONSTERS

Another wild walk with such unique writers as

**Saul Bellow
Chandler Brossard
George P. Elliott
Joseph Heller**

Front wrapper for A8.1.a

Dangs" by George P. Elliott, "Peacetime" by Brock Brower, "The Shores of Schizophrenia" by Hughes Rudd, "Day of the Alligator" by James Blake, "Address by Gooley MacDowell to the Hasbeens Club of Chicago" by Saul Bellow, "The Closing of This Door Must be Oh, So Gentle" by Chandler Brossard, "Entropy" by Thomas Pynchon, "The House of the Hundred Grassfires" by Algren. See A 13.

Typography and paper: 5¹³⁄₁₆" (6¹⁄₁₆") × 3⁷⁄₁₆". 40 lines per page. Running heads: rectos, story titles; versos, authors. Wove paper.

Binding: Front wrapper: '[figure in alley between two brick walls] [white] LANCER [horsehead] ORIGINAL 73-409 60¢ | [brilliant yellow (#83)] Nelson | Algren's | OWN BOOK OF | [very reddish orange (#34)] LONESOME | MONSTERS | [white] Another wild walk with such | unique writers as | [brilliant yellow] Saul Bellow | Chandler Brossard | George P. Elliott | Joseph Heller | [white] includes the complete text of the famous short | novel "AMONG THE DANGS" plus a remarkable | introduction and new story by the editor'. Spine printed on white background: '[black] LANCER | 73-409 | 60¢ | [vertically in strong yellowish green (#131)] NELSON ALGREN'S own book of LONESOME MONSTERS | [horizontal black horsehead]'. Back wrapper: photo of Algren and list of contributors. All edges trimmed and stained dark grayish green (#151).

Publication: Undetermined number of copies published in 1962. #73-409. 60¢. No copyright certificate.

Printing: Undetermined.

Location: MJB, Lilly.

Note: "The House of the Hundred Grassfires" was deleted from *A Walk on the Wild Side* before publication.

A 8.1.b
First edition, second printing: New York: Lancer, [1972].

#33016-125. Wrappers. $1.25.

A 8.2
Second edition, only printing: [New York]: Bernard Geis Associates, [1963].

Clothbound in dust jacket. $4.95. 15 stories: adds "South's Summer Idyll" by Terry Southern and "The Sleep of Baby Filbertson" by James Leo Herlihy.

A 8.3.a
First English edition, first printing

NELSON ALGREN'S
BOOK OF LONESOME
MONSTERS

A PANTHER BOOK

A 8.3.a: 4¼″ × 6¾″

NELSON ALGREN'S
BOOK OF LONESOME MONSTERS

A Panther Book

First published in the U.S.A.
by Lancer Books, Inc.

PRINTING HISTORY
Lancer edition published 1962
Panther edition published, February 1964

Conditions of Sale. This book shall not, without the written consent of the Publishers first given, be lent, re-sold, hired out or otherwise disposed of by way of trade in any form of binding or cover other than that in which it is published.

Printed in England by Hunt, Barnard & Co., Ltd.,
at the Sign of the Dolphin, Aylesbury, Bucks, and
published by Hamilton & Co. (Stafford), Ltd.,
108 Brompton Road, London, s.w.3

[1–6] 7–206 [207–208].

Perfect binding.

Contents: p. 1: blurb; p. 2: blank; p. 3: title; p. 4: copyright; p. 5: contents; p. 6: permissions; pp. 7–10: "The Book of Lonesome Monsters A Preface"; pp. 11–206: text; pp. 207–208: ads.
   13 stories: same contents as Lancer edition.

Typography and paper: 5⁷⁄₁₆″ (5⅝″) × 3⁷⁄₁₆″. 35 lines per page. Running heads: rectos, story titles; versos, authors. Wove paper.

Binding: Front wrapper, spine, and back printed on black background. Front: '[medium gray (#265) panther head in black circle and black '3'6' in medium gray circle] | [medium gray] Panther | [nude male figure] | [light purplish pink (#249)] NELSON ALGREN'S BOOK | OF LONESOME MONSTERS | [medium purple (#223)] A WILD WALK WITH [light purplish pink] SAUL | BELLOW, JOSEPH HELLER | GEORGE P. ELLIOTT □ □ □'. Spine: '[vertically in deep reddish orange (#36)] NELSON ALGREN'S book of lonesome MONSTERS | [horizontally] [black 'PB' in medium purple circle] | [medium purple panther head in black circle] | [white] 1627'. Back: '[deep reddish orange] These | exciting stories | by some of the most | talented writers of | contemporary fiction are a | terrifying testimonial | to the realization | that we are all | monsters, and always | alone | [medium purple] 'A COMMON TIE UNITES | THE STRANGLER OF A CHILD, | THE CREATIVE ARTIST, THE CLASSIC EROTICIST AND THE | MURDERER IN FICTION □ □''. All edges trimmed.

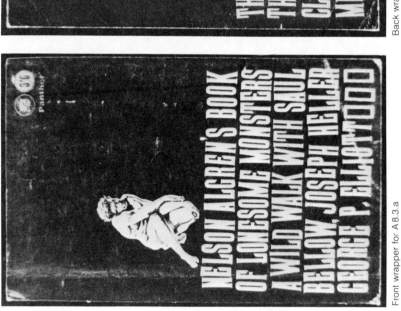

Back wrapper for A.8.3.a

Front wrapper for A.8.3.a

Publication: Undetermined number of copies published 27 February 1964.

Printing: See copyright page.

Locations: BL (5 FEB 64), MJB.

A 9 WHO LOST AN AMERICAN?

A 9.1.a
First edition, first printing (1963)

NELSON ALGREN

WHO

LOST

AN

AMERICAN?

THE MACMILLAN COMPANY—NEW YORK

A 9.1.a: 5⅝″ × 8¼″

THE AUTHOR WISHES TO THANK THE FOLLOWING PUBLICATIONS FOR PER-
MISSION TO REPRINT ARTICLES: "Rapietta Greensponge, Girl Counselor, Comes
to My Aid," first published in *Harlequin* under the title "Nobody Knows
My Name." "You Have Your People and I Have Mine," "The South of
England" and "There's Lots of Crazy Stuff in the Ocean" (under the title
"Moon of the Backstretch, Still and White") were first published in *Rogue;*
"The Bright Enormous Morning" was first published in *Rogue* under the
title "The Bride Below the Black Coiffure"; © Rogue Magazine/Greenleaf
Publishing Company 1961. "The Peseta with the Hole in the Middle" ap-
peared originally in *The Kenyon Review.* "The Night-Colored Rider,"
originally appeared in *Playboy,* under the title "The Father and Son Cigar";
© 1962 by Nelson Algren. "Down With All Hands," first published in *The
Atlantic Monthly.* "They're Hiding the Ham on the Pinball King," first
published in *Contact.* "When a Muslim Makes His Violin Cry, Head for the
Door," first published in *Nugget Magazine.*
      PERMISSION TO QUOTE FROM THE FOLLOWING PUBLICATIONS HAS BEEN
GRANTED BY THE PUBLISHERS: "Cocktails for Two" by Arthur Johnston and
Sam Coslow, Copyright © 1934 by Famous Music Corporation; Copyright
renewed 1961 by Famous Music Corporation. Passage from *Green Hills of
Africa* reprinted with the permission of Charles Scribner's Sons from *Green
Hills Of Africa* by Ernest Hemingway. Copyright 1935 Charles Scribner's
Sons. Selection from "An Impolite Interview with Hugh Hefner," in *The
Realist,* May 1961. Excerpt (page 57) from *Borstal Boy* by Brendan Behan,
Alfred A. Knopf, Inc. "Tricks Out of Times Long Gone" by Nelson Algren
first appeared in *The Nation,* September 1962. Excerpts from "Playboy's
Number One Playboy" by Peter Meyerson, *Pageant.* Excerpt from *The
Hive* by Camilo Cela, Farrar, Straus and Company, Inc. Excerpt from
Chicago Sun-Times reprinted with permission.

[A–B] [i–vi] vii–viii [ix–x] 1–337 [338–340]

[1–11]¹⁶

Contents: pp. A–B: blank; p. 1: half title; pp. ii–iii: title; p. iv: copyright; p. v:
'FOR SIMONE DE BEAUVOIR'; p. vi: blank; pp. vii–viii: contents; p. 1: half
title; p. 2: blank; pp. 3–337: text; pp. 338–340: blank.

14 essays: "New York: Rapietta Greensponge, Girl Counselor, Comes to
my Aid" (C 104, C 114), "Down With All Hands: The Cruise of the SS Meyer
Davis" (C 86), "The Banjaxed Land: You Have Your People and I Have Mine"
(C 100), "The South of England: They Walked Like Cats That Circle and
Come Back" (C 91), "Paris: They're Hiding the Ham on the Pinball King *or*
Some Came Stumbling" (C 92, C 98), "Barcelona: The Bright Enormous Morn-
ing" (C 97), "Almería: Show Me a Gypsy and I'll Show You a Nut" (C 109),
"Seville: The Peseta with the Hole in the Middle" (C 111), "Crete: There's Lots

Dust jacket for A 9.1.a

of Crazy Stuff in the Ocean" (C 102), "Istanbul: When a Muslim Makes his Violin Cry, Head for the Door" (C 106), "Chicago I: The Night-Colored Rider" (C 110), "Chicago II: If You Got the Bread You Walk,"* "Chicago III: If I Can't Sell It I'll Keep Settin' On It; I Jest Won't Give It Away,"* "Chicago IV: The Irishman in the Grotto, The Man in the Iron Suit, and The Girl in Gravity-Z: The Playboy Magazine Story *or* Mr. Peepers as Don Juan."* Asterisks indicate previously unpublished essays.

Typography and paper: 6³⁄₁₆″ (6⅜″) × 3¹³⁄₁₆″. 34 lines per page. Running heads: rectos, section titles; versos, 'WHO LOST AN AMERICAN?' Wove paper.

Binding: 3-piece binding; dark red (#16) paper-covered boards and yellowish gray (#93) V cloth (smooth). Front: '[deep green (#142)] WHO | LOST | [dark blue (#183)] AN AMERICAN?'. Spine: '[vertically in dark red] WHO LOST AN AMERICAN? [vertically in dark green] NELSON | ALGREN | [horizontally in dark blue] *Macmillan*'. Bottom and fore-edges untrimmed. Top edge stained medium red (#15). White endpapers.

Dust jacket: Front and spine printed on black background. Front: '[pinwheel in red, white, and blue] | [white] NELSON | aLGREN | [red] WHO LOST | [2 white stars] [red] aN [2 white stars] | [red] aMERICaN | [blue]? | [white] *A WHIRLIGIG SPIN THROUGH PARIS AND | PLAYBOY CLUBS, NEW YORK PUBLISHING | AND DUBLIN PUBS, CRETE AND CHICAGO •* | *AND MANY OTHER PHENOMENAL PLACES •* | *WITH THE AUTHOR OF* [red] *THE MAN WITH THE | GOLDEN ARM* [14 white stars]'. Spine: '[vertically] [white] NELSON | aLGREN [red] WHO LOST aN aMERICaN [blue]? [horizontally in white] Macmillan'. Back has photo of Algren by Stephen Deutch. Front and back flaps have blurb and note on Algren.

Publication: Undetermined number of copies published 13 May 1963. $5.95. Copyright #634004.

Printing: Produced by American Book—Stratford Press, New York.

Locations: MJB (dj), Lilly (dj).

A 9.1.b
First edition, second printing: New York: Macmillan, [1963].

Copyright page: 'SECOND PRINTING, 1963'.

A 9.1.c
First edition, only English printing

NELSON ALGREN

WHO
LOST
AN
AMERICAN?

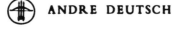 ANDRE DEUTSCH

A 9.1.c: 5⅜″ × 8⅜″

THE AUTHOR WISHES TO THANK THE FOLLOWING PUBLICATIONS FOR PER-
MISSION TO REPRINT ARTICLES: "Rapietta Greensponge, Girl Counselor, Comes
to My Aid," first published in *Harlequin* under the title "Nobody Knows
My Name." "You Have Your People and I Have Mine," "The South of
England" and "There's Lots of Crazy Stuff in the Ocean" (under the title
"Moon of the Backstretch, Still and White") were first published in *Rogue*;
"The Bright Enormous Morning" was first published in *Rogue* under the
title "The Bride Below the Black Coiffure"; © Rogue Magazine/Greenleaf
Publishing Company 1961. "The Peseta with the Hole in the Middle" appeared originally in *The Kenyon Review*. "The Night-Colored Rider," originally
appeared in *Playboy*, under the title "The Father and Son Cigar"; © 1962
by Nelson Algren. "Down With All Hands," first published in *The Atlantic
Monthly*. "They're Hiding the Ham on the Pinball King," first published in
Contact. "When a Muslim Makes His Violin Cry, Head for the Door," first
published in *Nugget Magazine*. "Dad Among the Troglodytes, Or, Show Me
a Gypsy and I'll Show You a Nut," first published in *The Noble Savage* No. 5.
"Shlepker, Or, White Goddess Say No Go That Part of Forest," first published
in *Cavalier*.

PERMISSION TO QUOTE FROM THE FOLLOWING PUBLICATIONS HAS BEEN
GRANTED BY THE PUBLISHERS: "Cocktails for Two" by Arthur Johnston and
Sam Coslow, Copyright © 1934 by Famous Music Corporation; Copyright
renewed 1961 by Famous Music Corporation. Passage from *Green Hills of
Africa* reprinted with the permission of the Executors of the Ernest Hemingway
Estate and Jonathan Cape Ltd. from *Green Hills of Africa* by Ernest Heming-
way. Selection from "An Impolite Interview with Hugh Hefner," in *The
Realist*, May 1961. Excerpt (page 57) from *Borstal Boy* by Brendan Behan,
Hutchinson & Co. Ltd. "Tricks Out of Times Long Gone" by Nelson Algren
first appeared in *The Nation*, September 1962. Excerpts from "Playboy's
Number One Playboy" by Peter Meyerson, *Pageant*. Excerpt from *The Hive*
by Camilo Cela, Farrar, Straus and Company, Inc. Excerpt from *Chicago
Sun-Times* reprinted with permission.

Same pagination as Macmillan printing.

[1] 2–11^{16}

Contents: Same as Macmillan printing.

Typography and paper: Same as Macmillan printing.

Binding: Deep reddish orange (#36) paper-covered boards with V pattern (smooth). Spine goldstamped: 'WHO LOST | AN | AMERICAN? | [rule] | Nelson | Algren | [bow-and-arrows device] | ANDRE | DEUTSCH'. All edges trimmed. White endpapers.

Dust jacket: Front and spine printed on black background. Front: '[white] WHO LOST AN AMERICAN? | by Nelson Algren [green] □ author of | The Man with the Golden Arm | [night scene in red, green, and white]'. Spine: '[white] WHO LOST | AN | AMERICAN | ? | [green] Nelson | Algren | [red and green swirl] | [white] [bow-and-arrows device] | André Deutsch'. Back: 'Some of our Novels' [18 titles]. Front flap: blurb. Back flap: photo of Algren by Stephen Deutch and biographical note.

Publication: Undetermined number of copies published in October 1963. 15s.

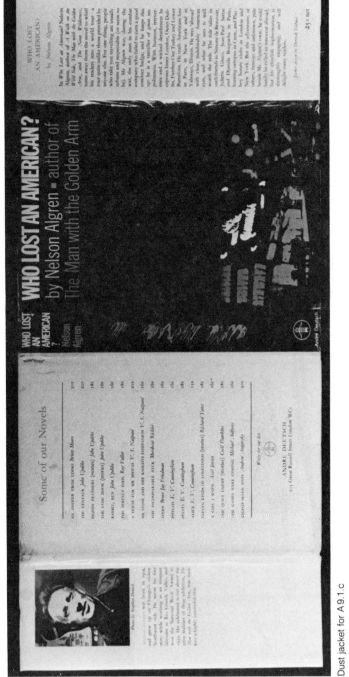

Dust jacket for A9.1.c

Printing: See copyright page.

Locations: BL (27 SEP 63), MJB (dj), Lilly (dj).

Advance review copy: Macmillan sheets sewn but unbound. Rubber-stamped on front: '[within single rule frame] ADVANCE AMERICAN COPY | PROBABLE PUB. DATE [holograph: '11/10/63'] | [stamped] APPROX. PRICE [holograph: '21/–'] | [stamped] ANDRE DEUTSCH LTD. | 105 GREAT RUSSELL ST. | LONDON, W.C.1'. Location: USC.

A 9.2.a
Second edition, first printing: [London]: Mayflower-Dell, [1965].

#9535. Wrappers. 5s.

A 10 CONVERSATIONS WITH NELSON ALGREN (brochure)

A 10
First edition, only printing (1964)

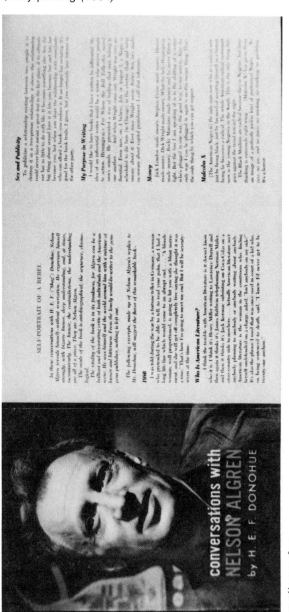

A 10: 5¹¹⁄₁₆″ × 8³⁄₁₆″

[1–6]

Single leaf folded twice.

Contents: p. 1: black-and-white photo of Algren; pp. 2–6: excerpts from *Conversations with Nelson Algren.*

Location: MJB.

A 11 CONVERSATIONS WITH NELSON ALGREN

A 11.1
First edition, only printing (1964)

CONVERSATIONS

WITH Nelson Algren

BY H. E. F. DONOHUE

 HILL AND WANG • NEW YORK

A 11.1: 5⅜″ × 7¹⁵⁄₁₆″

[A–B] [i–vi] vii–ix [x] xi–xii [1–2] 3–98 [99–100] 101–167 [168–170] 171–191 [192–194] 195–243 [244–246] 247–333 [334–338]

[1–11]^{16}

Contents: pp. A–B: blank; p. i: half title; p. ii: blank; p. iii: title; p. iv: copyright; p. v: 'Nelson Algren and H. E. F. Donohue | dedicate this book to | C.M.A.D.'; p. vi: blank; pp. vii–ix: 'Foreword' by Donohue; p. x: blank; pp. xi–xii: contents; p. 1: part title; p. 2: blank; pp. 3–98: text; p. 99: part title; p. 100: blank; pp. 101–167: text; p. 168: blank; p. 169: part title; p. 170: blank; pp. 171–191: text; p. 192: blank; p. 193: part title; p. 194: blank; pp. 195–243: text; p. 244: blank; p. 245: part title; p. 246: blank; pp. 247–330: text; pp. 331–333: 'Notes'; pp. 334–338: blank. See C 117, C 127.

Typography and paper: 5^{15}⁄₁₆" (6¼") × 3^{15}⁄₁₆"; 33 lines per page. Running heads: rectos, chapter titles; versos, 'CONVERSATIONS WITH NELSON ALGREN'. Wove paper.

Binding: Strong bluish green (#160) V cloth (smooth). Spine goldstamped: 'Conver- | sations | with | Nelson | Algren | • | DONOHUE | [h w device] | HILL | AND | WANG'. All edges trimmed. Top edge stained medium bluish green (#164). White headbands and footbands. White endpapers.

Dust jacket: Front: against photo of Algren '[white] conversations with | [red] NELSON ALGREN | [white] by H. E. F. DONOHUE. Spine printed on white background: '[black] DONOHUE | [vertically in red] conversations with | NELSON ALGREN | [horizontally in black] [h w device] | HILL | AND | WANG'. Back: 'Self-Portrait of a Rebel' [excerpts from book]. Front flap has blurb; continued on back flap with photo of Donohue.

Publication: Undetermined number of copies published 26 October 1964. $6.50. Copyright #A 765142.

Printing: Produced by American Book—Stratford Press, New York City.

Locations: LC (NOV 24 1964), MJB (dj), Lilly (dj), PSt.

Dust jacket for A11.1

A 11.2
Second edition, only printing: [New York]: Berkley, [1965].

Berkley Medallion #S1134. Wrappers. 75¢.

A 12 NOTES FROM A SEA DIARY

A 12.1.a
First edition, first printing (1965)

NOTES FROM
A SEA DIARY:

Hemingway All The Way

NELSON ALGREN

G. P. Putnam's Sons, New York

A 12.1.a: 5⅝″ × 8¼″

[1–10] 11–39 [40] 41–45 [46] 47–95 [96] 97–111 [112–114] 115–141 [142] 143–158 [159–160] 161–171 [172] 173–179 [180] 181–189 [190–192] 193–211 [212] 213–251 [252] 253–254 [255–256]

[1–8]^{16}

Contents: p. 1: half title; p. 2: card page [10 titles]; p. 3: title; p. 4: copyright; p. 5: *'For Max Geismar';* p. 6: blank; p. 7: acknowledgments; p. 8: blank; p. 9: *'Prefatory';* p. 10: blank; pp. 11–39: text; p. 40: blank; pp. 41–45: text; p. 46: blank; pp. 47–95: text; p. 96: blank; pp. 97–111: text; p. 112: blank; p. 113: *'Port of Bombay';* p. 114: blank; pp. 115–141: text; p. 142: blank; pp. 143–158: text; p. 159: *'Night in the Gardens | of Horn & Hardart';* p. 160: blank; pp. 161–171: text; p. 172: blank; pp. 173–179: text; p. 180: blank; pp. 181–189: text; p. 190: blank; p. 191: *'The Quais of Calcutta';* p. 192: blank; pp. 193–211: text; p. 212: blank; pp. 213–251: text; p. 252: blank; pp. 253–254: *'Epilogue: Quais of Calcutta';* pp. 255–256: blank. See C 75, C 88, C 101, C 103, C 113, C 122, C 130, C 163, C 206.

Typography and paper: 6½"(6⅞") × 4". 33 lines per page. Running heads: rectos, chapter titles; versos, 'NOTES FROM A SEA DIARY'. Wove paper.

Binding: Deep blue (#179) V cloth (smooth). Front blindstamped with Indian idol. Spine goldstamped: 'NOTES | FROM | A SEA | DIARY | *Hemingway | All the Way* | [leaf] | NELSON | ALGREN | *Putnam'*. Top edge trimmed; fore-edge untrimmed; bottom edge rough-trimmed. Strong blue (#178) endpapers.

Dust jacket: Front and spine printed against black background. Front: '[red rule] | [white] NELSON | ALGREN | [yellow script] Notes from a Sea Diary: | Hemingway all the way | [red rule] | [yellow] by the author of THE MAN WITH THE GOLDEN ARM | [blue Indian idol]'. Spine vertically: '[light yellow script] Notes from a Sea Diary [white] ALGREN [red] PUTNAM'. Photo of Algren by Jeff Lowenthal on back. Front and back flaps have blurb.

Dust jacket for A 12.1.a

Publication: Undetermined number of copies published 11 August 1965. $4.95. Copyright #A 813310.

Printing: Produced by Van Rees Book Bindery, New York.

Locations: LC (DEC 13 1965), MJB (dj), Lilly (dj), PSt.

A 12.1.b
First edition, first English printing (1966)

NOTES FROM A SEA DIARY:

Hemingway All The Way

NELSON ALGREN

André Deutsch

A 12.1.b: 5⅜" × 8⁷⁄₁₆"

Same pagination as first American printing.

[A] B–H^{16}

Contents: Same as first American printing.

Typography and paper: Same as first American printing.

Binding: Black paper-covered boards with V pattern (smooth). Spine silver-stamped: '[chain] | NOTES | FROM | A SEA | DIARY | [chain] | NELSON | ALGREN | [bow-and-arrows device] | ANDRE | DEUTSCH'. All edges trimmed. White endpapers.

Dust jacket: Front printed on white: '[6 drawings in black, red, light blue] [red] Nelson | Algren | [black] Notes from a Sea Diary | : Hemingway | all the way | [light blue] BY THE | AUTHOR OF | THE MAN | WITH THE | GOLDEN ARM'. Spine: '[red] Nelson | Algren | [black] Notes | from a | Sea | Diary | [light blue drawing continued from front] | [black bow-and-arrows device] | [red] ANDRE | DEUTSCH'. Back: ads and blurbs for *The Neon Wilderness* and *Who Lost an American?* Front and back flaps: blurb for *Notes from a Sea Diary.*

Publication: Undetermined number of copies published September 1966. 30s.

Printing: See copyright page.

Locations: BL (2 SEP 66), USC (dj), MJB (2 copies—dj), Lilly (dj).

Note: One MJB copy has lines 5–6, 9–12 on the copyright page hand-canceled in ink.

A 12.2
Second edition, only printing: Greenwich, Conn.: Fawcett Crest, [1966].

#R973. Wrappers. 60¢.

Dust jacket for A 12.1.b

A 12.3
Third edition, only printing: [London]: Mayflower-Dell, [1967].

#6491-8. Wrappers. 5s.

A 13 THE LAST CAROUSEL

A 13.1
First edition, only printing (1973)

THE LAST

CAROUSEL

G. P. Putnam's Sons, New York

A 13.1: 5⅜″ × 8⅛″

[i–xii] 1–435 [436]

[1–19]^{16}

Contents: p. i: half title; pp. ii–iii: title; p. iv: copyright; p. v: *'For Kay Boyle';* p. vi: blank; p. vii–viii: contents; pp. ix–x: acknowledgments; p. xi: half title; p. xii: blank; pp. 1–435: text; p. 436: blank.

37 stories, essays, and poems: "Dark Came Early in That Country" (C 139), "Could World War I Have Been a Mistake?" (C 158), "Otto Preminger's Strange Suspenjers" (B 28), "I Never Hollered Cheezit the Cops" (C 168), "The Mad Laundress of Dingdong-Daddyland" (C 143), "The Leak That Defied the Books" (C 147), "Tinkle Hinkle and the Footnote King" (C 75), "Hand in Hand Through the Greenery with the grabstand clowns of arts and letters,"* "Come in If You Love Money,"* "Brave Bulls of Sidi Yahya" (C 174), "I Know They'll Like Me in Saigon" (C 141), "Airy Persiflage on the Heaving Deep" (B 27), "No Cumshaw No Rickshaw" (C 162), "Letter from Saigon" (C 142, C 144), "What Country Do You Think You're In?"* "Police and Mama-sans Get It All" (C 159), "Poor Girls of Kowloon" (C 145), "After the Buffalo" (B 26), "The Cortez Gang,"* "The House of the Hundred Grassfires" (A 8), "Previous Days" (C 154, C 166), "Epitaph: *The Man with the Golden Arm*" (A 4, C 38), "The Passion of Upside-Down-Emil: A Story From Life's Other Side" (C 122, C 150), "Merry Christmas Mr. Mark" (C 46), "I Guess You Fellows Just Don't Want Me" (C 163), "Everything Inside Is a Penny" (B 19, C 110, C 167), "The Ryebread Trees of Spring" (C 84), "Different Clowns for Different Towns" (C 153), "Go! Go! Go! Forty Years Ago" (C 76, C 77, C 78), "Ballet for Opening Day: The Swede Was a Hard Guy" (C 30), "A Ticket on Skoronski" (C 135), "Ode to an Absconding Bookie" (C 173), "Bullring of the Summer Night" (C 149), "Moon of the Arfy Darfy" (C 125, C 149), "Watch Out for Daddy" (C 66), "The Last Carousel" (C 164), "Tricks Out of Times Long Gone" (C 108). Asterisks indicate previously unpublished material.

Typography and paper: 6¾" (7¹⁄₁₆") × 4⅛". 41 lines per page. No running heads. Wove paper.

Binding: Light gray (#264) V cloth (smooth). Spine: '[very red (#11)] *The Last* | *Carousel* | [brilliant blue (#177)] NELSON | ALGREN | [line of devices] | [very red] *PUTNAM*'. All edges trimmed. White endpapers.

Dust jacket for A 13.1

Dust jacket: Front and spine printed on purple background. Front: '[white] NELSON | ALGREN | [light blue] Author of MAN WITH THE GOLDEN ARM | [white, curved] THE LAST CAROUSEL | [color photo of carousel horses]'. Spine: '[white] THE | LAST | CAROUSEL | [light blue] NELSON | ALGREN | [white] PUTNAM'. Back: photo of Algren by Stephen Deutch. Front and back flaps have blurb.

Publication: Undetermined number of copies published 28 November 1973. $8.95. Copyright #A 494830.

Printing: Produced by Colonial Press, Clinton, Mass.

Locations: LC (JAN 14 1974), MJB (dj), Lilly (dj), PSt.

Advance review copy: Sheets bound in olive-green paper wrappers. Printed paper label on front: 'G. P. Putnam's Sons | 200 MADISON AVENUE, NEW YORK, N.Y. 10016 | [rule] | NOTE: This is UNCORRECTED PROOF | *Title* [typed] THE LAST CAROUSEL | [printed] *Author* [typed] Nelson Algren | [printed] *Classification* [typed] fiction | [printed] *Probable publication date* [typed] October 31, 1973 | [printed] *Probable price* [typed] $8.95 | [printed] *Illustrations* [typed] none | [printed] *Approximate length* [typed] 512 pages | [printed] [rule] | REVIEWERS: Please check all quotations against the final bound | book, since changes may be made in this proof copy.' Location: USC. A set of galleys is in the collection of Paul and Elizabeth Garon.

A 13.2
Second edition, only printing: [New York]: Warner, [1975].

#79-727. Wrappers. $1.95. Copyright page: 'First Printing, February, 1975'.

A 14 CALHOUN [THE DEVIL'S STOCKING]

A 14.1.a
First edition, first printing (1981)

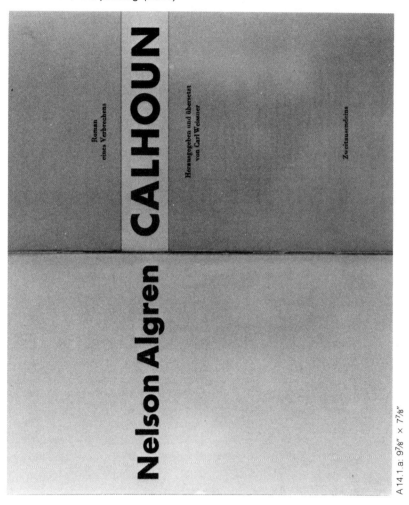

A 14.1.a: 9⅞" × 7⅞"

```
1. Auflage, 1.-5. Tausend, Oktober 1981.
Die deutsche Ausgabe folgt dem Originalmanuskript
in der Fassung vom Oktober 1980.
Arbeitstitel: THE DEVIL'S STOCKING.
Copyright © 1981 by Nelson Algren.
Welterstausgabe.
Copyright © 1981 by Zweitausendeins.
Postfach, D-6000 Frankfurt am Main 61,
für die deutsche Übersetzung.
Alle Rechte vorbehalten, insbesondere das Recht des Nachdrucks
in Zeitschriften oder Zeitungen, des öffentlichen Vortrags,
der Verfilmung oder Dramatisierung, der Übertragung durch Rundfunk
oder Fernsehen, auch einzelner Textteile.
Satz und Druck bei Laupp & Göbel, Tübingen.
Papier von Scheufelen, Oberlenningen.
Gebunden bei G. Lachenmaier, Reutlingen.
Produktion Greno GmbH, D-6053 Obertshausen 2.
Printed in Germany.
U.S.A.: Whoever wants to order this book can do so at
Blue Angel, Inc., 1738 Allied Street, Charlottesville, VA 22901.
Dieses Buch gibt es nur bei Zweitausendeins
im Versand (Postfach, D-6000 Frankfurt am Main 61)
oder in den Zweitausendeins-Läden in Berlin, Frankfurt, Freiburg,
Hamburg, Hannover, Köln, München, Saarbrücken, Wiesbaden.
```

[i–vi] vii–xi [xii] [1–2] 3–376 [377–380]

[1]⁴ [2–25]⁸

Contents: p. i: half title; pp. ii–iii: title; p. iv: copyright; p. v: 'Für Steve'; p. vi: photo of Algren and Wolf Wondratschek; pp. vii–xii: 'VORWORT' by Wondratschek; p. 1: half title; p. 2: blank; pp. 2–277: text, headed 'I | ERSTER PROZESS'; pp. 378–380: blank. See C 214, C 215.

Typography and paper: 6" (6⁵⁄₁₆") × 3⅜". 34 lines per page. No running heads. Wove paper.

Binding: Very red (#11) vinyl. Front: '[black] CALHOUN | [on medium gray (#265) square within black frame] NELSON | ALGREN | WERKE | Zweitausendeins'. Spine: '[black, vertically up] CALHOUN | [horizontally on medium gray square within black frame] NELSON | ALGREN | WERKE | Zweitausendeins'. All edges trimmed. Top edge sprinkled in black. Black ribbon. Black head and footbands. White endpapers.

Dust jacket: None.

Publication: 5,000 copies published October 1981. 20 DM.

Printing: See copyright page.

Location: Jan Herman.

A 14.1.b
First edition, second printing: [Frankfurt am Main]: Zweitausendeins, [1982].

Copyright page: '2. Auflage, 6.–10. Tausend, Januar 1982.' Location: MJB.

Binding for A 14.1.a

A 14.2.a
First English-language edition, first printing (cloth and wrappers, 1983)

Library of Congress Catalogue Card Number: 83–45249

ISBN: 0-87795-548-4
Hardcover Edition: 0-87795-547-6

Manufactured in the United States of America

10 9 8 7 6 5 4 3 2 1

This book is printed on acid free paper. The paper in this book meets the guidelines for permanence and durability of the Committee on Production Guidelines for Book Longevity of the Council on Library Resources.

[i–x] [1] 2–5 [6–9] 10–12 [13–15] 16–115 [116–119] 120–168 [169–171] 172–181 [182–185] 186–194 [195–197] 198–216 [217–219] 220–234 [235–237] 238–259 [260–263] 264–278 [279–281] 282–308 [309–310]

Not sewn.

Copyright page: Publisher's printing code in cloth and paperbound copies: '10 9 8 7 6 5 4 3 2 1'.

Contents: p. i: half title; p. ii: card page; p. iii: title; p. iv: copyright; p. v: 'To Stephen Deutch'; p. vi: disclaimer; pp. vii–viii: contents; p. ix: acknowledgment to the National Endowment for the Arts; p. x: blank; pp. 1–5: 'Foreword | by Herbert Mitgang'; p. 6: blank; p. 7: 'The Last Interview | by | W. J. Weatherby'; p. 8: blank; pp. 9–12: interview; p. 13: '[rule] | I | [rule] | First | Trial'; p. 14: blank; pp. 15–308: text; p. 309: cat sketch; p. 310: blank.

ISBN: 0-87795-547-6 $16.95

The Devil's Stocking

NELSON ALGREN

Foreword by Herbert Mitgang
The Last Interview by W. J. Weatherby

The last, heretofore unpublished, novel by America's novelist, *The Man with the Golden Arm*, *A Walk on the Wild Side* and other American classics.

Here is the world Nelson Algren knew intimately and about which he writes with intense feeling for the denizens of society's underside: a world of pimps, prostitutes, prisoners, the shadowy arena of high- and low-purse boxing; a place where Blacks, Sicilians, cops, con artists walk one another with literary and brutal purpose. Centered on this dark stage, with the vagaries of the law as backdrop, a boxer who is in cool with the language as he is deadly with his fists becomes the victim of a revengeful dupe—and with manly pride takes the final, harrowing count.

The Devil's Stocking sustains a great literary reputation, capstone of a long and brilliant career.

(continued on back flap)

NELSON ALGREN

A NOVEL

The Devil's Stocking

The Devil's Stocking   NELSON ALGREN

The Devil's Stocking

"In this new novel, I've tried to write about a man's struggle against injustice—that's the only story worth telling. I've written it from my guts."—Nelson Algren

"*The Devil's Stocking* is all Algren. The wisdom of turning fact into fiction becomes apparent immediately, for the novel at its best brings into play the author's imagination, his stacked and sometimes familiar deck of urban jacks and queens and street guerillas.... Certainly the characters he has created speak for themselves, and always in authentic tones. The subterranean world that he knew so well as any living American writer is here.... Maybe the author is forcing us to look at what he perceives to be injustice in the dark recesses of the American Way. If so, *The Devil's Stocking* is muckraking in a strong literary tradition."
—from the Foreword by Herbert Mitgang.

"The man one met on the last day reflected exactly the writer one had read in all the books ranging from *The Man with the Golden Arm* to *The Devil's Stocking* and that is an exceedingly rare literary achievement. It means that as long as his books are read, the man will never die—that downright, excitable, aggressive, but, deep down, gentle man known as Nelson Algren."
—from the Last Interview by W. J. Weatherby

ISBN: 0-87795-547-6

NELSON ALGREN's works include *Somebody in Boots*, *Never Come Morning*, *The Neon Wilderness*, *Chicago: City on the Make*, *A Walk on the Wild Side*, as well as the internationally acclaimed *The Man with the Golden Arm*. Shortly before his death in May, 1981, Nelson Algren was elected to the National Institute and Academy of Arts and Letters.

Jacket design by Paul Bacon
Author photo by Stephen Deutch

Arbor House Publishing Company
235 East 45th Street
New York, N.Y. 10017

Printed in U.S.A.   9-83

Dust jacket for A 14.2.a

Typography and paper: 6⅝″ (6¹⁵⁄₁₆″) × 4⁵⁄₁₆″. No running heads. Wove paper.

Cloth binding: Medium yellowish brown (#77) V cloth (smooth). Spine gold-stamped: '[vertically] [single rules above and below author's name] | NEL-SON | ALGREN | *The Devil's Stocking* [horizontal torch device]'. Medium yellowish brown and white headbands and footbands. All edges trimmed. White endpapers.

Dust jacket: Tan background. Front: '[dark brown] [torch device in upper left corner with 6 lines of type] The | ARBOR HOUSE | LIBRARY OF | CONTEM-PORARY | AMERICANA | [rule] | NELSON | ALGREN | [thick rule] A NOVEL [thick rule] | [dark red] *The Devil's Stocking*'. Spine: '[vertically] [dark red] *The Devil's Stocking* [dark brown] NELSON ALGREN [horizontal torch device with 6 lines of type as above] | [leaf]'. Back: Boxed 3-line statement by Algren and excerpts from Mitgang foreword and Weatherby interview. Front flap has blurb for *The Devil's Stocking*. Back flap has photo of Algren by Stephen Deutch and biographical note.

Wrappers: Front and spine same as dust jacket. Back cover retains Algren, Mitgang, and Weatherby material; but adds 'Cover design by Paul Bacon', torch device, publisher's imprint, and 'Printed in U.S.A. 9-83'. Inside front wrapper has photo of Algren by Stephen Deutch and biographical note citing Algren as the author of *Puss in Boots*. Inside back cover has blurb for *The Devil's Stocking*. All edges trimmed. See introduction for comment on bindings.

Publication: Undetermined number of copies simultaneously published in cloth and wrappers, 30 September 1983. Cloth: $16.95 (ISBN: 0-87795-547-6). Wrappers: $8.95 (ISBN: 0-87795-548-4). No copyright certificate.

Printing: Undetermined.

Locations: Cloth: Paul and Elizabeth Garon (dj), MJB (dj); wrappers: MJB (review slip).

A 14.2.b
Second printing: New York: Arbor House, [1983].

Copyright page: '10 9 8 7 6 5 4 3 2'. Clothbound.

Proof copy: Orange wrappers printed in black. Front: 'On September 1, 1983 | Arbor House Will Publish Nelson Algren's Last Novel | [following 6 lines within rules frame] NELSON | ALGREN | [thick rule] | *The | Devil's | Stocking* | [torch device with 6 lines of type outside frame] | PUBLICATION: September | PRICE: $16.95, cloth | $9.95, paperback | UNCORRECTED PROOFS | THE ARBOR HOUSE LIBRARY OF | CONTEMPORARY AMERICANA'. Spine: '[vertically] Algren's *The Devil's Stocking* [horizontal torch device with 6 lines of type]'. Produced by Crane Duplicating Service, Barnstable, Mass. Location: MJB.

Algren's bookplate

B. First Appearances in Books

B1 O. HENRY MEMORIAL AWARD
1935

O. HENRY | MEMORIAL AWARD | [swash] Prize Stories of 1935 | [roman] SELECTED AND EDITED BY | HARRY HANSEN | *Literary Editor* | *of The New York World-Telegram* | [DD anchor device] | DOUBLEDAY, DORAN & COMPANY, INC. | GARDEN CITY, NEW YORK | 1935

On Copyright page: 'FIRST EDITION'.

"The Brothers' House," pp. 61–67. See C 11. Collected in *The Neon Wilderness.*

B2 GALENA GUIDE
1937

American Guide Series | [rule] | GALENA GUIDE | Compiled and Written by | FEDERAL WRITERS' PROJECT (ILLINOIS) | Works Progress Administration | [decoration] | Sponsored by | THE CITY OF GALENA | 1937

Wrappers.

Anonymous. On the annotated contents page of MJB copy Algren claims to have provided the titles for "Many Mines," "Many Miners," "Boom Border," "The Fermenting Fifties," and "Armed Years." Next to "A Middle-Aged Clerk in a Faded Army Coat," he notes: "I wrote this by hand—Algren." But Algren's inscription in the Ohio State University copy claims that he wrote eight chapters: "Burial Ground," "Many Mines," "Many Miners," "Boom Border," "Lead and Grain," "The Fermenting Fifties," "A Middle-Aged Clerk in a Faded Army Coat," and "Armed Years." See Kenneth G. McCollum, *Nelson Algren A Checklist,* p. 43; C 161; and Robert A. Tibbetts, "Nelson Algren and the *Galena Guide:* A Further Note," *Serif,* 9 (Fall 1972), 48.

B3 O. HENRY MEMORIAL AWARD
1941

O. HENRY MEMORIAL AWARD | *PRIZE STORIES* | OF | *1941* | [decorated rule] | SELECTED AND EDITED BY | HERSCHEL BRICKELL | [decorated rule] | [DD ship device] | DOUBLEDAY, DORAN AND COMPANY, INC. | GARDEN CITY *1941* NEW YORK

95

On Copyright page: 'FIRST EDITION'.

"A Bottle of Milk for Mother," pp. 69–89. The headnote on p. 70 quotes Algren. See C 26 for "Biceps."

A new edition of this volume was published with the imprint of The Book League of America (1941?).

The story was reprinted as "Biceps" in *The Best American Short Stories 1942,* ed. Martha Foley (Boston: Houghton Mifflin, 1942) and collected in *The Neon Wilderness* as "A Bottle of Milk for Mother."

B 4 MODERN READING
1943

MODERN | *READING* | *NUMBER SEVEN* | *EDITED BY* | *REGINALD MOORE* | [stag] | *LONDON:* | *WELLS GARDNER, DARTON & CO. LTD.*

1943. Big Ben Books. Wrappers.

"The Captain Is a Card," pp. 9–18. See C 31.

B 5 A TREASURY OF AMERICAN FOLKLORE
1944

A TREASURY OF | AMERICAN | *FOLKLORE* | *STORIES, BALLADS, AND* | *TRADITIONS OF THE PEOPLE* | *Edited by* | B. A. BOTKIN | *In Charge of The Archives of American Folk Song of the Library of Congress* | *with a Foreword by* | CARL SANDBURG | [drawing of alligator with horse's head] | CROWN PUBLISHERS | NEW YORK

1944.

"Hank, the Free Wheeler," pp. 540–542.

B 6 THE BEST AMERICAN SHORT STORIES
1945

THE | *Best* | AMERICAN | SHORT STORIES | 1945 | [decorated rule] | *and The Yearbook of the American Short Story* | *Edited by* | MARTHA FOLEY | [Forum Books device] | THE WORLD PUBLISHING COMPANY | CLEVELAND AND NEW YORK

1946.

On copyright page: 'First Printing October 1946'.

"How The Devil Came Down Division Street," pp. 1–7. See C 35. Collected in *The Neon Wilderness.*

B 7 CROSS SECTION
1947

CROSS | SECTION | ◊ 1947 ◊ | ◊ | *A collection of* | *new American writing* | *edited by* | *EDWIN SEAVER* | ◊ ◊ | ◊ | SIMON AND SCHUSTER, NEW YORK

1947.

"Single Exit," pp. 217–224.

B 8 PRIZE STORIES OF 1950
1950

[2-page title: left] DOUBLEDAY & COMPANY, INC., GARDEN CITY, NEW YORK, 1950 [right] prize | stories | of | 1950 | [anchor device] | the | O. Henry Awards | SELECTED AND EDITED BY HERSCHEL BRICKELL

On copyright page: 'First Edition'.

"The Captain Is Impaled," pp. 52–67. See C 41.

B 9 AMERICAN NOVELISTS OF TODAY
1951

[decorated A] AMERICAN NOVELISTS | OF TODAY | [rule] | [script] Harry T. Warfel | [roman] AMERICAN BOOK COMPANY | [script] New York Cincinnati Chicago Boston | Atlanta Dallas San Francisco

1951.

Quotes Algren, p. 8.

B 10 AMERICA DAY BY DAY
1953

[on two-page diary] *America day by day* | *by Simone de Beauvoir* | *Grove Press   New York*

1953.

Quotes Algren, pp. 104, 107, 306.

B 11 TWENTIETH CENTURY AUTHORS FIRST SUPPLEMENT
1955

TWENTIETH CENTURY | AUTHORS | FIRST SUPPLEMENT | A Biographical Dictionary of Modern Literature | *Edited by* | STANLEY J. KUNITZ | *Assistant*

Editor | VINETA COLBY | [beacon device] | NEW YORK | THE H. W. WILSON
COMPANY | NINETEEN HUNDRED FIFTY-FIVE

Quotes Algren, pp. 14–15.

B 12 THE WRITER OBSERVED
1956

HARVEY BREIT | The Writer Observed | [W P seal] | THE WORLD PUBLISH-
ING COMPANY | CLEVELAND AND NEW YORK

1956.

On copyright page: 'FIRST EDITION'.

Interview with Algren, pp. 85–87. See C 42.

B 13 NEW WORLD WRITING
1956

New | WORLD | WRITING | NINTH MENTOR SELECTION | PUBLISHED BY
[arrow device] | THE NEW AMERICAN LIBRARY

1956.

On copyright page: '*First Printing, April, 1956*'.

Wrappers. #MD 170. "Beasts of the Wild," pp. 66–71. Prepublication excerpt
from *A Walk on the Wild Side.*

B 14 THE RACE FOR SPACE!
1957

The Race For Space ! | [planets] | JOSEPH SORREN   PAUL G. NEIMARK |
publisher   editor

Chicago: Camerarts, 1957. Wrappers.

"Ain't Nobody on My Side?" p. 13.

B 15 WRITERS AT WORK
1958

[within frame consisting of decorative rule at top and bottom and single rules
at sides] Writers | at | Work | The *Paris Review* Interviews | Edited, and with an

Introduction, by | MALCOLM COWLEY | [decoration] | NEW YORK : The Viking Press : MCMLVIII | [rule and decorated rule]

Algren interview with Alston Anderson and Terry Southern, pp. 233–249; facsimile of revised typescript page from *A Walk on the Wild Side,* p. 232. See C 59.

B 16 THE PERMANENT PLAYBOY
1959

THE | PERMANENT | PLAYBOY | Edited by Ray Russell | Crown Publishers, Inc., New York

1959.

"All Through the Night," pp. 419–429. See C 66.

B 17 THE 1950's
1960

THE | 1950's | *America's "Placid" Decade* | [3 squares] | *Edited by* | Joseph Satin | MOORHEAD STATE COLLEGE | HOUGHTON MIFFLIN COMPANY • BOSTON | [gothic] The Riverside Press Cambridge

1960.

" 'Chicago is a Wose,' " pp. 177-178. See C 73.

B 18 THE SEVEN STAIRS
1962

Stuart Brent | THE | Houghton Mifflin Company Boston | SEVEN | The Riverside Press Cambridge | STAIRS | Nineteen Sixty-Two

Letter from Algren to Otto Preminger, pp. 47–48.

B 19 THE BEDSIDE PLAYBOY
1963

THE | BEDSIDE | PLAYBOY | EDITED BY HUGH M. HEFNER | PLAYBOY PRESS | ¶ [rabbit] P

1963.

"The Father and Son Cigar," pp. 97–111. See C 110, C 167. Collected as "Everything Inside Is a Penny" in *The Last Carousel.*

B 20 F. S. C.
1963

[2-page title] F. S. C. | a Novel Book original | by | CON SELLERS | (author of *Born of Battle*) | cover illustration | by | Arnie Kohn

Chicago: Novel Books, 1963. #6081. 60¢. Wrappers.

Introduction by Algren, pp. 1–2.

Location: USC.

B 21 ERIK DORN
1963

[swash] ERIK DORN | [roman] A NOVEL BY BEN HECHT | *Introduction by NELSON ALGREN* | [rule] | THE UNIVERSITY OF CHICAGO PRESS | CHICAGO AND LONDON

1963.

"Erik Dorn A Thousand and One Afternoons in Nada," pp. vii–xvii. See C 120.

B 22 TABOO
1964

[left] seven short stories | which no publisher | would touch | from seven | leading writers | a New Classics House original | [right, vertically] TABOO

Chicago: New Classics House, 1964. #7N730. Wrappers.

"The Daddy of Them All," pp. 31–59.

Location: USC.

B 23 FORCE OF CIRCUMSTANCE
1965

SIMONE DE BEAUVOIR | FORCE OF | CIRCUMSTANCE | TRANSLATED FROM THE FRENCH | By Richard Howard | [GPPS seal] | G. P. PUTNAM'S SONS | NEW YORK

1965.

Quotes Algren throughout: cable, p. 162; letter, p. 184. See C 155.

B 24 AUTHORS TAKE SIDES ON VIETNAM
1967

[short vertical rule] | AUTHORS | TAKE SIDES ON VIETNAM | Two questions on the war in Vietnam | answered by the authors of several nations | EDITED BY | CECIL WOOLF AND JOHN BAGGULEY | [device] | PETER OWEN • LONDON

1967.

Statement by Algren, pp. 75–76.

Location: BL (29 AUG 1967)

AUTHORS | TAKE | SIDES | ON VIETNAM | Two Questions | on the War in Vietnam | Answered by the Authors | of Several Nations | Edited by | CECIL WOOLF and | JOHN BAGGULEY | [device] SIMON AND SCHUSTER, NEW YORK

1967.

On copyright page: 'FIRST PRINTING'. Wrappers.

Statement by Algren, p. 17.

Note: Separate editions; contents differ. London edition precedes; New York edition published October 1967.

B 25 YEARS OF PROTEST
1967

YEARS OF | PROTEST | A Collection of American Writings of the 1930's | edited by Jack Salzman | BARRY WALLENSTEIN, ASSISTANT EDITOR | PEGASUS [device] NEW YORK

1967.

"A Place to Lie Down," pp. 347–353. See C 13.

B 26 THE TRUE STORY OF BONNIE & CLYDE
1968

THE TRUE STORY | OF | BONNIE & CLYDE: | AS TOLD BY BONNIE'S MOTHER AND | CLYDE'S SISTER | *Former title:* FUGITIVES | [rule] | *With an Introduction by* NELSON ALGREN | *Compiled, Arranged, and Edited by* | JAN I. FORTUNE | [oval Signet seal] | A SIGNET BOOK | Published by The New American Library

1968.

On copyright page: 'FIRST PRINTING, FEBRUARY, 1968'. Wrappers.

"Introduction," pp. v–xix. Collected as "After the Buffalo" in *The Last Carousel.*

B 27 WORKS IN PROGRESS
1970

WORKS IN | PROGRESS | NUMBER ONE | Book trade distributed by | Doubleday & Company, Inc. | The Literary Guild of America, Inc. | New York, N.Y.

1970. Wrappers.

"Airy Persiflage on the Heaving Deep," pp. 87–97. Collected in *The Last Carousel.*

B 28 FOCUS
1972

FOCUS | MEDIA | EDITORS | JESS RITTER | SAN FRANCISCO STATE COLLEGE | GROVER LEWIS | CHANDLER PUBLISHING COMPANY | An Intext Publisher | SAN FRANCISCO • SCRANTON • LONDON • TORONTO

1972.

"Otto Preminger's Strange Suspenjers," pp. 10–18. Collected in *The Last Carousel.*

B 29 THE DREAM AND THE DEAL
1972

THE DREAM | AND THE DEAL | The Federal Writers' Project, 1935–1943 | [photo of shelf of books] | *by Jerre Mangione | Little, Brown and Company——Boston—Toronto*

1972.

On copyright page: 'FIRST EDITION'.

Statement by Algren, pp. 121, 123.

B 30 NELSON ALGREN   A CHECKLIST
1973

[2-page title] REN NELSON ALGREN NELSON ALGREN NELSON ALGREN NELSON ALGREN NELSON ALGREN | [left: drawing of Algren] | [right] A

CHECKLIST | Compiled by | Kenneth G. McCollum | Introduction | by | Studs Terkel | [device] A BRUCCOLI ◇ CLARK BOOK | PUBLISHED BY GALE RESEARCH COMPANY, BOOK TOWER, DETROIT, 1973

Facsimiles of letters, inscriptions, and revised typescript for "Salomon and Morris: Two Patriots of the Revolution," pp. 87–107.

B 31 WRITERS IN REVOLT
1973

WRITERS | *in* | *REVOLT* | The Anvil Anthology | *Edited by JACK CONROY* | *and CURT JOHNSON* | LAWRENCE HILL and COMPANY | New York • Westport

1973. Cloth and wrappers.

On copyright page: 'First edition: November 1973'.

"A Holiday in Texas," pp. 1–7. See C 6.

"Within the City," pp. 8–9. See C 17.

"Makers of Music," p. 209. See C 20.

"Program for Appeasement," pp. 210–211. See C 22.

B 32 A 'CATCH-22' CASEBOOK
1973

[2-page title] [left] Thomas Y. Crowell Company [tyc monogram] New York, Established 1834 | [right: 5 slanted lines] edited by Frederick Kiley | UNITED STATES AIR FORCE ACADEMY | A 'CATCH-22' CASEBOOK | and Walter McDonald | TEXAS TECH UNIVERSITY

1973.

On copyright page: '1 2 3 4 5 6 7 8 9 10'.

"The Catch," pp. 3–5. See D 138, E 3.

B 33 NELSON ALGREN
1975

NELSON ALGREN | By MARTHA HEASLEY COX | San Jose State University | and | WAYNE CHATTERTON | Boise State University | [eagle] | TWAYNE PUBLISHERS | A DIVISION OF G. K. HALL & CO., BOSTON

1975.

Quotes previously unpublished interviews and letters; also "Worldshaker," "The Man on Wheels," "This Life We've Led," "The Room with the Low-Knobbed Door." See A 7.

B 34 SELF-PORTRAIT
1976

[rule] | SELF-PORTRAIT | [rule] | Book People Picture Themselves | *From the collection of* | BURT BRITTON | *Random House* [device] *New York* | [rule] 1976.

Self-caricature with inscription, p. 10.

B 35 DICTIONARY OF LITERARY BIOGRAPHY
1981

Dictionary of Literary Biography • Volume Nine | American Novelists, 1910–1945 | Part 1: Louis Adamic–Vardis Fisher | Edited by James J. Martine | *Saint Bonaventure University* | Foreword by Orville Prescott | A Bruccoli Clark Book | Gale Research Company • Book Tower • Detroit, Michigan 48226 | 1981

Kenneth G. McCollum, "Nelson Algren," pp. 10–15. Quotes letter, p. 11.

B 36 THE WORLD ACCORDING TO BRESLIN
1984

The World | *According to Breslin* | *Jimmy Breslin* [thick and thin horizontal rules] | ANNOTATED BY Michael J. O'Neill | AND William Brink | *Ticknor & Fields* NEW YORK 1984

On copyright page: 'S 10 9 8 7 6 5 4 3 2 1'.

"The Man in a $20 Hotel Room," pp. 270–273. Interview. See C 196.

C. First Appearances in Magazines and Newspapers—Exclusive of Reviews

It was Algren's custom to revise, rewrite, or recast material from periodical publication to book publication—and from book to book. This section notes the most significant of these recyclings.

C 1
"So Help Me," *Story,* 3 (August 1933), 3–14.

Story. Collected in *The Neon Wilderness.*

C 2
"Forgive Them, Lord," *A Year Magazine,* #2 (December 1933–April 1934), 144–149.

Story.

C 3
"For the Homeless Youth of America," *Masses,* #12 (March–April 1934), 4.

Article. Cited as "from his novel *Native Son*" but not incorporated in *Somebody in Boots.*

C 4
"If You Must Use Profanity," *American Mercury,* 31 (April 1934), 430–436.

Story. Prepublication excerpt from *Somebody in Boots.*

C 5
"Buffalo Sun," *The Calithump,* 1 (April 1934), 13–14.

Story. Prepublication excerpt from *Somebody in Boots.*

C 6
"Holiday in Texas," *The Anvil,* 6 (May–June 1934), 23–26.

Story. See B 31.

C 7
"Lest the Traplock Click," *The Calithump,* 1 (June 1934), 21–30.

Story.

C 8
"Kewpie Doll," *The Anvil,* 7 (July–August 1934), 26–27.

Story. Prepublication material from *Somebody in Boots* rewritten in first-person narrative. Also summarized in *A Walk on the Wild Side,* pp. 45–46.

C 9
" 'Politics' in Southern Illinois," *The New Republic,* 79 (1 August 1934), 307.

Unsigned article by Algren.

C 10
"Storm in Texas," *Partisan Review,* 1 (September–October 1934), 26–29.

Story. Substantially revised prepublication excerpt from *Somebody in Boots.*

C 11
"The Brothers' House," *Story,* 5 (October 1934), 22–25.

Story. See B 1. Collected in *The Neon Wilderness.*

C 12
"Call for an American Writers' Conference," *The New Masses,* 14 (22 January 1935), 20.

Public statement signed by Algren and others.

C 13
"A Place to Lie Down," *Partisan Review,* 2 (January–February 1935), 3–9.

Story. Substantially revised prepublication excerpt from *Somebody in Boots.* See B 25.

C 14
"Winter in Chicago," *The Anvil,* 2 (May–June 1935), 27–29.

Story. Prepublication excerpt from *Somebody in Boots.*

C 15
"A Lumpen," *The New Masses,* 16 (2 July 1935), 25–26.

Story.

C 16
"American Obituary," *Partisan Review,* 2 (October–November 1935), 26–27.

Article.

C 17
"Within the City," *The Anvil,* 3 (October–November 1935), 9.

Article. See B 31.

C 18
"Thundermug," *The Windsor Quarterly,* 2 (Winter 1935), 206–229.

Prepublication excerpt of chapter 9 from *Somebody in Boots.* Most of the copies of this issue have blank pages for "Thundermug" with the explanation,

"Censored by Commonwealth College." A few copies with the material were surreptitiously printed. See McCollum, *Nelson Algren A Checklist,* pp. 50–52.

C 19
"Federal Art Projects: WPA: Literature," *The Chicago Artist,* 1 (December 1937–January 1938), 6, 10.

Article.

C 20
"Makers of Music," *The New Anvil,* 1 (March 1939), 23.

Verse. See B 31.

C 21
"Utility Magnate," *The New Anvil,* 1 (April–May 1939), 16–17.

Verse. Published under pseudonym Lawrence O'Fallon. The masthead of this issue lists Algren as managing editor.

C 22
"Program for Appeasement," *The New Anvil,* 1 (June–July 1939), 12.

Verse. See B 31.

C 23
"Home and Goodnight," *Poetry,* 55 (November 1939), 74–76.

Verse.

C 24
"Travelog," *Poetry,* 55 (November 1939), 76–77.

Verse.

C 25
"This Table On Time Only," *Esquire,* 13 (March 1940), 78–79.

Verse.

C 26
"Biceps," *Southern Review,* 6, #4 (1941), 713–728.

Story. See B 3. Collected as "A Bottle of Milk for Mother" in *The Neon Wilderness.* A substantially revised version of the story appears in the chapter "Only Myself to Blame," *Never Come Morning.*

C 27
"Local South," *Poetry,* 58 (September 1941), 308–309.

Verse.

C 28
"How Long Blues," *Poetry,* 58 (September 1941), 309.

Verse.

C 29
"Stickman's Laughter," *Southern Review,* 7, #4 (1942), 845–851.

Story. Revised for *The Neon Wilderness.*

C 30
"The Swede Was a Hard Guy," *Southern Review,* 7, #4 (1942), 873–879.

Verse. Substantially revised for *The Last Carousel.*

C 31
"The Captain Is a Card," *Esquire,* 17 (June 1942), 50–51, 162–163.

Story. See B 4.

C 32
"He Swung and He Missed," *The American Mercury,* 55 (July 1942), 57–63.

Story. Collected in *The Neon Wilderness.*

C 33
"Do It the Hard Way," *The Writer,* 56 (March 1943), 67–70.

Article.

C 34
"The Children," *The American Mercury,* 57 (September 1943), 310–314.

Story. Collected in *The Neon Wilderness.*

C 35
"How the Devil Came Down Division Street," *Harper's Bazaar,* 78 (May 1944), 106–107.

Story. See B 6. Collected in *The Neon Wilderness.*

C 36
"The Face on the Barroom Floor," *The American Mercury,* 64 (January 1947), 26–35.

Story. Revised for *The Neon Wilderness.* Also recycled in *A Walk on the Wild Side.*

C 37
"Laughter in Jars—Not as Sandburg Wrote of It," *Chicago Sun Book Week* (20 July 1947), 2.

Article.

C 38

"Epitaph: *The Man with the Golden Arm,*" *Poetry,* 70 (September 1947), 316–317.

Verse. Reprinted in *The Man with the Golden Arm* and *The Last Carousel.*

C 39

"Authors Defend Open Letter," *New York Times* (24 May 1948), 18.

Public letter signed by Algren and others.

C 40

"Chicago Author Looks at French Culture—and Finds It to Be Mostly American," *Chicago Sun-Times Book Week* (26 June 1949), 8X.

Article.

C 41

"The Captain Is Impaled," *Harper's Magazine,* 199 (August 1949), 88–96.

Story. See B 8. Material recycled in *The Man with the Golden Arm.*

C 42

Harvey Breit, "Talk with Nelson Algren," *New York Times Book Review* (2 October 1949), 33.

Interview. See B 12.

C 43

Les Brown, "Algren a Sociable Guy—Socially Conscious Writer," *Roosevelt* [University] *Torch* (24 October 1949), 5.

Interview.

C 44

Dick Bauer, "States Ideas and Ideals—Has No Social Solutions," *Roosevelt* [University] *Torch* (24 October 1949), 5, 7–8.

Interview.

C 45

"Algren Depicts Dire Straits, Hopeless Resignation of Italy," *Roosevelt* [University] *Torch* (14 November 1949), 5.

Article.

C 46

"Merry Christmas, Mr. Mark!" *Chicago Sunday Tribune Magazine of Books* (4 December 1949), 3.

Article. Collected in *The Last Carousel.*

C 47

"What Is America Reading?" *Northwestern University Reviewing Stand,* 13 (29 January 1950), 3–10.

Transcription of a radio panel discussion in which Algren participated.

C 48

"Headliners and Bestsellers," *New York Times Book Review* (11 June 1950), 5.

Article. Quotes Algren.

C 49

Bernard Gavzer, "Noted Author Insists Cheap Flat Suits Him Fine," *Bergen* [New Jersey] *Evening Record* (18 August 1950), 4.

Interview.

C 50

"What Are You Doing Out There?" *New York Times* (15 January 1951), 9.

Public statement signed by Algren and others.

C 51

"One Man's Chicago," *Holiday,* 10 (October 1951), 72–73, 75, 77–78, 80–83, 86–87, 89, 117, 119–120.

Article. Substantially revised for *Chicago: City on the Make.*

C 52

"Some of the Authors of 1951, Speaking for Themselves," *New York Herald Tribune Book Review* (7 October 1951), 27.

Statement.

C 53

"Things of the Earth: A Groundhog View," *The California Quarterly,* 2 (Autumn 1952), 3–11.

Speech. See C 220.

C 54

Van Allen Bradley, "Author Nelson Algren—He Sits and Broods," *Chicago Daily News* (6 September 1952), 24.

Interview.

C 55

"Great Writing Bogged Down In Fear, Says Novelist Algren," *Chicago Daily News* (3 December 1952), 44.

Article. Reprinted as "American Christmas, 1952," *The Nation,* 175 (27 December 1952), inside cover and 588.

C 56
"Hollywood Djinn with a Dash of Bitters," *The Nation,* 177 (25 July 1953), 68–70.

Article.

C 57
"Editors Write," *Trace: A Chronicle of Living Literature,* 2 (October 1953), 16–18.

Includes Algren statement.

C 58
"Eggheads Are Rolling: The Rush to Conform," *The Nation,* 177 (17 October 1953), 306–307.

Article.

C 59
Alston Anderson and Terry Southern, "Nelson Algren," *Paris Review,* 3 (Winter 1955), 36–58.

Interview. See B 15.

C 60
Luther Nichols, "An Author Explains His Views," *San Francisco Examiner Modern Living* (20 May 1956), 14.

Interview.

C 61
Sidney Fields, "Only Human," *New York Daily Mirror* (11 June 1956), 24.

Interview.

C 62
William F. Michelfelder, " 'Golden Arm' Author has Mean Elbow," *New York World-Telegram & The Sun* (22 June 1956), 17.

Interview.

C 63
"Mr. Goodbuddy and the Mighty Dripolator," *Nugget,* 1 (July 1956), 4–5, 47, 75.

Story. Revised prepublication excerpt from *A Walk on the Wild Side,* pp. 120–131.

C 64
"Lovers, Sec-fiends, Bugs in Flight," *Nugget,* 1 (October 1956), 20–22.

Story. Revised prepublication excerpt from *A Walk on the Wild Side,* pp. 302–319.

C 65
George Murray, "Author of 'The Man with the Golden Arm' Takes a Walk Amid His Old West Side Haunts," *Chicago American Pictorial Living* (7 October 1956), 6–7.

Interview.

C 66
"All Through the Night," *Playboy,* 4 (April 1957), 29, 69–72.

Story. See B 16. Reprinted as middle section of "Watch Out for Daddy," *The Last Carousel.*

C 67
"G-String Gomorrah," *Esquire,* 48 (August 1957), 47–48.

Article.

C 68
Robert A. Perlongo, "Interview with Nelson Algren," *Chicago Review,* 11 (Autumn 1957), 92–98.

C 69
"4 Intellects Discourse On State Of Culture Here," *Chicago Sun-Times* (22 November 1957), 18.

Quotes Algren. See C 217.

C 70
"Come Back, Little Sheba," *Chicago Sun-Times* (27 November 1957), 19.

Unsigned editorial. Quotes Algren.

C 71
"Say a Prayer for the Guy," *Manhunt,* 6 (June 1958), 31–35.

Story.

C 72
"Good-By to Old Rio," *Esquire,* 50 (August 1958), 80–81.

Story. Revised for preface to *Somebody in Boots* (1965). See A 1.5.

C 73
" 'Chicago Is a Wose,' " *The Nation,* 188 (28 February 1959), 191.

Article. See B 17.

C 73a

"Kup's Column," *Chicago Sun-Times* (15 March 1959), sec. 1, p. 60.

Statement.

C 74

David Ray, "A Talk on the Wild Side: A Bowl of Coffee with Nelson Algren," *The Reporter,* 20 (11 June 1959), 31–33.

Interview. Reprinted as "Talk on the Wild Side," *Cavalcade,* 4 (July 1964), 52–55.

C 75

"Ding-Dong, Tinkle Hinkle, The Finkified Lasagna and The Footnote King," *Dial,* 1 (Fall 1959), 125–131.

Article. Substantially revised as "July 6th: South China Sea, Two Days from the Port of Hong Kong. Dingding, Hinkletinkle, the Finkified Lasagna and the Man Too Timid to Damn," *Notes from a Sea Diary.* Also substantially revised as "Tinkle Hinkle and the Footnote King," *The Last Carousel.*

C 76

"Nelson Algren Writes Impressions of Series," *Chicago Sun-Times,* final edition (2 October 1959), 5.

Article. Revised and incorporated in "Go! Go! Go! Forty Years Ago," *The Last Carousel.*

C 77

"Algren Writes of Roses and Hits," *Chicago Sun-Times,* final edition (3 October 1959), 5.

Article. Revised and incorporated in "Go! Go! Go! Forty Years Ago," *The Last Carousel.*

C 78

"Nelson Algren's Reflections: Hep-Ghosts of the Rain," *Chicago Sun-Times,* final home edition (10 October 1959), 12. In final edition as "Algren at Game 6: Shoeless Joe Is Gone, Too," sec. 2, p. 12.

Article. Revised and incorporated in "Go! Go! Go! Forty Years Ago," *The Last Carousel.*

C 79

K. Allsop, "A Talk on the Wild Side," *Spectator,* 203 (16 October 1959), 509, 511.

Interview.

C 80
"The Chateau at Sunset or It's a Mad World, Master Copperfield," [Wayne State University] *Graduate Comment,* 3 (December 1959), 5–7, 12.

Speech.

C 81
"3 Tapes," *Writer's Yearbook,* 31 (1960), 45–49, 148, 150.

Interviews with Erskine Caldwell, Meyer Levin, and Algren.

C 82
"Nelson Algren's View," *Chicago Sun-Times* (31 January 1960), 11.

Letter.

C 83
"How the Man with the Record One Eighth of an Inch Long Was Saved by a Bessarabian Rye," *Esquire,* 53 (June 1960), 105.

Story.

C 84
"The Unacknowledged Champion of Everything," *The Noble Savage,* 2 (September 1960), 14–24.

Article. Revised as "The Ryebread Trees of Spring," *The Last Carousel.*

C 85
"The Mafia of the Heart," *Contact,* 2 (October 1960), 9, 11–15.

Article.

C 86
"Down With All Hands," *The Atlantic Monthly,* 206 (December 1960), 76, 81–84.

Article. Revised as "Down with All Hands: The Cruise of the SS Meyer Davis," *Who Lost an American?*

C 87
"Remembering Richard Wright," *The Nation,* 192 (28 January 1961), 85.

Article. Recycled in "Let's See Your Hands," *Chicago Free Press,* 1 (2 November 1970), 25–27. See C 156.

C 88
" 'The Marquis of Kingsbury, You Could Have Him,' " *Gent,* 5 (February 1961), 48–49.

Story. Recycled in "July 9th: Concannon Gets the Ship in Trouble or Assy-end Up on Ho-Phang Road," *Notes from a Sea Diary.*

C 89
"Clear and Lucid Camus," *The Nation,* 192 (1 April 1961), inside front cover.

Letter.

C 90
"Contact!" *The Nation,* 192 (22 April 1961), inside front cover.

Letter.

C 91
"The South of England," *Rogue,* 6 (May 1961), 26–28, 60, 76.

Article. Substantially revised for "The South of England: They Walked Like Cats That Circle and Come Back," *Who Lost an American?*

C 92
"The Bride Below the Black Coiffure," *Rogue,* 6 (July 1961), 30–31.

Verse. Reprinted in "Paris: They're Hiding the Ham on the Pinball King *or* Some Came Stumbling," *Who Lost an American?* See C 98.

C 93
"He's Upsy-Downsy," *Rogue,* 6 (July 1961).

Letter.

C 94
"What Rexroth Thinks," *The Nation,* 193 (29 July 1961), 59.

Letter.

C 95
"Moon of the Backstretch: Still and White," *Rogue,* 6 (August 1961), 12–16, 24.

Article.

C 96
"Fellini's 'La Dolce Vita': A Discussion by Nelson Algren, Mario De Vecchi, and Studs Terkel," *wmft Chicago Fine Arts Guide,* 10 (August 1961), 5–9.

C 97
"The Peseta with the Hole in the Middle, Part I," *The Kenyon Review,* 23 (Autumn 1961), 549–570.

Article. Substantially revised as "Barcelona: The Bright Enormous Morning," *Who Lost an American?*

C 98
"They're Hiding the Ham on the Pinball King, or, Some Came Stumbling," *Contact,* 3 (September 1961), 101–111.

Article. Collected as "Paris: They're Hiding the Ham on the Pinball King *or* Some Came Stumbling," *Who Lost an American?* See C 92.

C 99
"To Horse," *Rogue,* 6 (October 1961).

Letter.

C 100
"You Have Your People and I Have Mine," *Rogue,* 6 (November 1961), 28–30, 58, 60, 78.

Article. Prepublication excerpt from "The Banjaxed Land: You Have Your People and I Have Mine," *Who Lost an American?*

C 101
"Hemingway: The Dye That Did Not Run," *The Nation,* 193 (18 November 1961), 387–390.

Article. Incorporated in "July 13th: Indian Ocean: 'I Can See You Have Been Wounded,' " *Notes from a Sea Diary.*

C 102
"The Moon of King Minos," *Rogue,* 7 (February 1962), 26ff.

Not seen. Possibly appears as "Crete: There's Lots of Crazy Stuff in the Ocean," *Who Lost an American?*

C 103
"God Bless the Lonesome Gas Man," *The Dude,* 6 (March 1962), 11–12, 73.

Story. Substantially revised as "Seven Feet Down and Creeping." See C 147. Recycled in "July 4th: East China Sea," *Notes from a Sea Diary.*

C 104
"The Role of the Writer in America," *Michigan's Literary Quarterly: Voices,* 2 (Spring 1962), 3–27.

Symposium with Vance Bourjailly, William Styron, Gore Vidal, and Algren. Parts of Algren's speech are revised and incorporated in "New York: Rapietta Greensponge, Girl Counselor, Comes to My Aid," *Who Lost an American?* See C 114.

C 105
Michael Edelstein and Robert Lamb, "No Room, No Time, No Breath for the Bessemer Processes of the Heart," *The University of Chicago Phoenix* (Spring 1962), 2–8.

Interview.

C 106
"Fabulous Istanbul Isn't the Town for Me," *Nugget,* 7 (June 1962), 31–32, 34, 66–67.

Article. Substantially revised as "Istanbul: When a Muslim Makes His Violin Cry, Head for the Door," *Who Lost an American?*

C 107
"Afternoon in the Land of the Strange Light Sleep," *Cavalier,* 12 (September 1962), 24–25, 27.

Article.

C 108
"Tricks Out of Times Long Gone," *The Nation,* 195 (22 September 1962), 162.

Verse. Substantially revised for *The Last Carousel.*

C 109
"Dad Among the Troglodytes, or Show Me a Gypsy and I'll Show You a Nut," *The Noble Savage,* 5 (October 1962), 59–64.

Article. Collected as "Almería: Show Me a Gypsy and I'll Show You a Nut," *Who Lost an American?*

C 110
"The Father and Son Cigar," *Playboy,* 9 (December 1962), 120–121, 186–188, 190, 192, 194.

Article. See B 19, C 167. Collected as "Everything Inside Is a Penny," *The Last Carousel.* Substantially revised as "Chicago I: The Night-Colored Rider," *Who Lost an American?*

C 111
"The Peseta with the Hole in the Middle, Part II," *The Kenyon Review,* 24 (Winter 1962), 110–128.

Article. Substantially revised as "Seville: The Peseta with the Hole in the Middle," *Who Lost an American?*

C 112
Bob Ellison, "A Walk on the Wild Side with Nelson Algren," *Fling* (January 1963), 13–14, 58–59.

Quotes Algren.

C 113
"Shlepker, or White Goddess Say You Not Go That Part of Forest," *Cavalier,* 13 (February 1963), 12–14, 84–89.

Story. A section of this story is incorporated in "Kanani Mansions," *Notes from a Sea Diary.*

C 114
"Whobody Knows My Name, or How to Be a Freedom-Rider Without Leaving Town," *Harlequin,* 1 (April 1963), 8–11, 45–46, 75–77.

Article. Revised as "New York: Rapietta Greensponge, Girl Counselor, Comes to My Aid," *Who Lost an American?* See C 104.

C 115
Fred J. Cook, "The Corrupt Society—Part II: Unexpected Rewards of Virtue," *The Nation,* 196 (1–8 June 1963), 453–496.

Quotes Algren letter, p. 455.

C 116
"Nelson Algren: Writer on the Wild Side," *Caper,* 9 (July 1963), 52–54, 59.

Not seen.

C 117
H.E.F. Donohue, "Nelson Algren Interviewed: The Writer as Child, Youth and Army Privateer," *The Carleton Miscellany,* 4 (Fall 1963), 3–36.

Prepublication excerpts from *Conversations with Nelson Algren.*

C 118
Norman Mailer, "The Big Bite," *Esquire,* 60 (September 1963), 16, 18, 20.

Quotes Algren.

C 119
Hendrik L. Leffelaar, "Nelson Algren Off the Cuff," *Cavalier,* 13 (November 1963), 80–82.

Interview.

C 120
Austin C. Wehrwein, "Hecht Attacks Algren Preface," *New York Times* (21 November 1963), 36.

Quotes Algren. See B 21.

C 121
Bob Ellison, "Three Best-Selling Authors: Conversations," *Rogue,* 8 (December 1963), 21, 23, 24, 78–79.

Interviews with Harper Lee, Willard Motley, and Algren.

C 122
"Stanley Upside Down Or: Why Trail Bullfighters When You Can Teach Iambic Pentameter?" *New York Herald Tribune Book Week* (8 December 1963), 1, 12, 14.

Article. Sections incorporated in "Upside-Down Emil." See C 150. Substantially revised as "July 14th: Rafts of a Summer Night," *Notes from a Sea Diary*.

C 123

"Revival in Chicago," *Newsweek*, 62 (9 December 1963), 94–96.

Quotes Algren.

C 124

Park Honan, "Nelson Algren Came Down Division Street," *New City*, 2 (15 January 1964), 11–13.

Quotes Algren.

C 125

"The Moon of the Arfy Darfy," *Saturday Evening Post*, 237 (26 September 1964), 44–45, 48–49.

Story. Collected in *The Last Carousel*.

C 126

Anne Pourtois, "Conversation Avec Nelson Algren," *Europe*, 52 (October 1964), 72–77.

Interview.

C 127

H.E.F. Donohue, "Nelson Algren at Fifty-Five," *The Atlantic Monthly*, 214 (October 1964), 79–80, 83–85.

Interview. Prepublication excerpt from *Conversations with Nelson Algren*.

C 128

Simone de Beauvoir, "An American Rendezvous: The Question of Fidelity, Part II," *Harper's*, 229 (December 1964), 111–114, 116, 119–120, 122. Excerpt from *Force of Circumstance*.

Quotes Algren. See B 23.

C 129

"I Ain't Abelard," *Newsweek*, 64 (28 December 1964), 58–59.

Interview.

C 130

"Hemingway All the Way," *Cavalier*, 15 (February 1965), 30–31.

Article. Expanded as "Prefatory," *Notes from a Sea Diary*.

C 131
"Down with Cops," *Saturday Evening Post,* 238 (23 October 1965), 10, 14.

Article. See C 157.

C 132
"A Letter," *The Carleton Miscellany,* 6 (Winter 1965), 104.

Letter to Erling Larsen.

C 133
Mike Royko, "A Small-Print Burglar Hustles Nelson Algren," *Chicago Daily News* (7 June 1966), 3.

Includes Algren letter.

C 134
"Nobody Knows," *The Saturday Review,* 49 (3 September 1966), 15.

Verse.

C 135
"A Ticket on Skoronski," *Saturday Evening Post,* 239 (5 November 1966), 48–49, 52–56.

Story. Collected in *The Last Carousel.*

C 136
Letter to David Laing, *Inscape* (Winter–Spring 1966), 63–64.

C 137
"The Emblems and the Proofs of Power," *The Critic,* 25 (February–March 1967), front cover and 20–25.

Letter to Joel Wells.

C 138
Robert Cromie, "Cromie Looks at Books and Authors: Algren's 'Finksville' Has Another Name," *Chicago Tribune* (16 February 1968), 23.

Quotes Algren.

C 139
"Home to Shawneetown," *The Atlantic Monthly,* 222 (August 1968), 41–47.

Story. Revised as "Dark Came Early in That Country," *The Last Carousel.*

C 140
Sylvan Fox, "McCarthy Offices Raided at Dawn by Chicago Police," *New York Times* (31 August 1968), 1, 11.

Quotes Algren.

C 141

"I Know They'll Like Me in Cholon," *The Critic,* 27 (February–March 1969), 58–61.

Article. Substantially revised as "I Know They'll Like Me in Saigon," *The Last Carousel.*

C 142

"That Was No Albatross," *The Critic,* 27 (April–May 1969), 58–59, 96.

Article. Material incorporated into "Letter from Saigon," *The Last Carousel.*

C 143

"Decline & Fall of Dingdong-Daddyland," *Commentary,* 48 (September 1969), 69–76.

Story. Collected as "The Mad Laundress of Dingdong-Daddyland," *The Last Carousel.*

C 144

"Letter from Saigon," *The Critic,* 28 (September–October 1969), 14, 94.

Article. One section is incorporated in "Letter from Saigon," *The Last Carousel.*

C 145

"They Don't Want to Belong to Us: Itinerant Journalist Goes Bamboo," *The Critic,* 28 (November–December 1969), 76–81.

Article. Collected as "Poor Girls of Kowloon," *The Last Carousel.*

C 146

John William Corrington, "Nelson Algren Talks with NOR's Editor-at-Large," *New Orleans Review,* 1 (Winter 1969), 130–132.

Interview.

C 147

"Seven Feet Down and Creeping," *New Orleans Review,* 2, #1 (1970), 3–5.

Story. See C 103. Collected as "The Leak That Defied the Books," *The Last Carousel.*

C 148

Phil Tracy, "Nelson Algren: One with His Own," *National Catholic Reporter,* 6 (1 April 1970), 6.

Quotes Algren.

C 149
"Get All the Money," *Playboy,* 17 (June 1970), 82, 84, 86, 98, 186–188, 191, 194, 197–198.

Story. Revised as "Bullring of the Summer Night," *The Last Carousel.* Verse from "Get All the Money" also incorporated in "Moon of the Arfy Darfy," *The Last Carousel.*

C 150
"Upside-Down Emil," *Chicago Free Press,* 1 (28 September 1970), 12–13.

Story. Collected as "The Passion of Upside-Down-Emil: A Story from Life's Other Side," *The Last Carousel.* See C 122.

C 151
"The Rest of the Way Is by the Stars," *Chicago Free Press,* 1 (5 October 1970), 22–27.

Article.

C 152
"A Ticket to Biro-Bidjan," *Chicago Free Press,* 1 (5 October 1970), 37–38.

Article.

C 153
"Early Chicago Journalism," *Chicago Free Press,* 1 (12 October 1970), 28–30.

Article. Revised as "Different Clowns for Different Towns," *The Last Carousel.*

C 154
"Previous Days," *Chicago Free Press,* 1 (19 October 1970), 30–31.

Article. Expanded for *The Last Carousel.* See C 166.

C 155
"Pottawattomie Ghosts," *Chicago Free Press,* 1 (26 October 1970), 26–29.

Article.

C 156
"Let's See Your Hands," *Chicago Free Press,* 1 (2 November 1970), 25–27.

Article. See C 87.

C 157
"The Cop Mentality," *Chicago Free Press,* 1 (9 November 1970), 27–28.

Article. Condensed from C 131.

C 158
"Swan Lake Re-Swum," *Audience,* 1 (January 1971), 10–11.

Article. Revised as "Could World War I Have Been a Mistake?" *The Last Carousel.*

C 159
"White Mice and Mama-sans Take It All," *Rolling Stone,* #83 (27 May 1971), 30–31.

Article. Collected as "Police and Mama-sans Get It All," *The Last Carousel.*

C 160
"No Cumshaw, No Rickshaw: Well, What Did You Expect? Pat Suzuki?" Part 1, *Holiday,* 49 (July–August 1971), 32–35, 79.

Article.

C 161
Dean H. Keller, "Nelson Algren and the *Galena Guide,*" *The Serif,* 8 (September 1971), 33–34.

Quotes Algren. See B 2.

C 162
"No Cumshaw, No Rickshaw," Part 2, *Holiday,* 50 (November 1971), 44–47, 77, 80.

Article. Collected in *The Last Carousel.*

C 163
"Ipso Facto," *Audience,* 1 (November–December 1971), 78–81.

Story. Collected as "I Guess You Fellas Just Don't Want Me," *The Last Carousel.* Material also recycled in "July 15th: Arabian Sea," *Notes from a Sea Diary.*

C 164
"The Last Carrousel," *Playboy,* 19 (February 1972), 72–74, 76, 126, 180, 182–186, 188, 190.

Story. Collected in *The Last Carousel.*

C 165
"Where Did Everybody Go?" *Chicago Tribune Magazine* (13 February 1972), 20, 22–25.

Article.

C 166
"Blanche Sweet Under the Tapioca," *Chicago Tribune Magazine* (30 April 1972), 42–45.

Article. Expanded as "Previous Days," *The Last Carousel.* See C 154.

C 167
"Down Memory Lane with Ann Esch and Nelson Algren," *Chicago Tribune Magazine* (18 June 1972), 25–26, 28, 30, 32, 36.

Letter to Esch. Material from "The Father and Son Cigar." See B 19, C 110.

C 168
"I Never Hollered Cheezit the Cops," *The Atlantic Monthly,* 230 (October 1972), 93–96.

Story. Collected in *The Last Carousel.*

C 169
"The Cockeyed Hooker of Bugis Street," *Chicago Tribune Magazine* (8 October 1972), 30.

Verse.

C 170
"The Country of Kai-Li," *Chicago Tribune Magazine* (8 October 1972), 29.

Verse.

C 171
"Gentlemen: The Law Is Present," *Chicago Tribune Magazine* (8 October 1972), 29.

Verse.

C 172
"It Don't Matter How You Spell It," *Chicago Tribune Magazine* (8 October 1972), 30.

Verse.

C 173
"Ode to an Absconding Bookie," *Chicago Tribune Magazine* (8 October 1972), 31.

Verse. Collected in *The Last Carousel.*

C 174
"The Way to Médenine," *Playboy,* 19 (December 1972), 153, 222, 234, 239–240.

Article. Collected as "Brave Bulls of Sidi Yahya," *The Last Carousel.*

C 175
"The Best Novels of World War II," *The Critic,* 31 (January–February 1973), 74–77.

Article. Reprinted as "Going After Glory War Reviews: The Best Novels of World War II," *The Washington Book Review,* 1 (July/August 1979), 2–3, 32–34.

C 176
Tom Fitzpatrick, "Some Blunt But Not Unkind Words from Nelson Algren," *Chicago Sun-Times* (26 March 1973), 14, 16.

Interview.

C 177
"A Good Place to Be From?" *Chicago Tribune Book World* (10 June 1973), 5.

Statement.

C 178
Henry Kisor, "Nelson Algren, Hale and Salty at 64," [*Chicago Daily News*] *Panorama* (27–28 October 1973), 2–3.

Interview.

C 179
John F. Baker, "Nelson Algren," *Publishers Weekly,* 204 (31 December 1973), 12–13.

Interview.

C 180
Jess Ritter, " 'The Dostoevski of Division Street,' " *Pacific Sun* (7–13 February 1974), 6, 15.

Interview.

C 181
"A Walk on the Mild Side Costs the Soul Plenty," *New York Times* (20 April 1974), 31.

Article.

C 182
Pete Waldmeir, "A Chat with 2 Authors," *Detroit News* (22 April 1974), 10D.

Interviews with James T. Farrell and Algren.

C 183
James David Harkness, "Nelson Algren: 60 Years from Mack Avenue, He Still Likes 'The People Underneath,' " [*Detroit Free Press*] *Detroit* (26 May 1974), 6–9.

Interview.

C 184
Michaela Tuohy, "A Day at the Races with Nelson Algren," *Chicago Tribune Magazine* (30 June 1974), 18–19, 22.

Quotes Algren.

C 185
Karen Nettles, "Algren Outgrows Image as Poet of the Slums," [Gainesville, Fla.] *Sun* (13 October 1974), F-4.

Quotes Algren.

C 185a
"Writers at Work (a Progress Report)," *The Critic,* 33 (October–November–December 1974), 64.

Statement.

C 186
Peter Richardson, "Nelson Algren: Teaching the New Rebels," [Gainesville, Fla.] *Sun* (17 November 1974), F-10.

Quotes Algren.

C 187
Michael Hirsley, " 'Golden Arm' Ambience Gone, Author Goes, Too," *Chicago Tribune* (3 February 1975), sec. 2, p. 1.

Quotes Algren.

C 188
Paul Gapp, "Algren's Final Chapter in the City on the Make," *Chicago Tribune* (10 February 1975), sec. 2, p. 4.

Quotes Algren.

C 189
Eleanor Randolph, "Algren Sale to Fund Move to 'Boom Town,' " *Chicago Tribune* (2 March 1975), 34.

Quotes Algren.

C 190
Eleanor Randolph, "Algren's House Sale not Quite a Best Seller," *Chicago Tribune* (9 March 1975), 10.

Quotes Algren.

C 191
Rick Soll, "Nelson Algren Bids Final Farewell," *Chicago Tribune* (10 March 1975), 2.

Quotes Algren.

C 192
"On Kreativ Righting," *New York Times* (29 March 1975), 23.

Article.

C 193
"Requiem," *Chicago,* 24 (September 1975), 120–124.

Article.

C 194
"Algren Decides to Live in Paterson," *New York Times* (29 September 1975), 61.

Quotes Algren.

C 195
Jim Gallagher, "Literary 'Exile' Is Pleasant for Algren," *Chicago Tribune* (29 March 1977), sec. 2, pp. 1, 4.

Interview.

C 196
Jimmy Breslin, "A Writer of the First Rank from the Second City," *New York Daily News* (16 May 1978), 4, 20.

Interview. See B 36.

C 197
"Topless in Gaza," *New York,* 11 (30 October 1978), 88–90.

Article.

C 198
Jan Herman, "Nelson Algren: The Angry Author," [*Chicago Sun-Times*] *Chicago Style* (21 January 1979), 8–11.

Quotes Algren.

C 199
" 'We Never Made It to the White Sox Game,' " *Chicago Tribune Book World* (2 September 1979), 1.

Article.

C 200
"Boycott TABA," *New York Review of Books,* 26 (11 October 1979), 54.

Open letter signed by Algren and others.

C 201

"There Will Be No More Christmases," *Chicago,* 29 (July 1980), 132–134.

Story.

C 202

Herbert Mitgang, "In This Corner, Algren," *New York Times Book Review* (17 August 1980), 31.

Quotes Algren.

C 203

"Impressions of Studs as Bogus Frenchman and Urban Thoreau," *Chicago Tribune Book World* (14 September 1980), 1, 5.

Article.

C 204

"Last Rounds in Small Cafés: Remembrances of Jean-Paul Sartre and Simone de Beauvoir," *Chicago,* 29 (December 1980), 210–213, 237–238, 240.

Article.

C 205

Randolph Hogan, "A Book Fair for Small Presses Opens in the 'Village,' " *New York Times* (27 March 1981), C-23.

Quotes Algren.

C 206

"A Few Rounds with Papa and a Bottle of Scotch," *Chicago Tribune Book World* (29 March 1981), 1, 6.

Article. Slightly revised episode from "June 27th: Lions, Lionesses, Deadbone Crunchers," *Notes from a Sea Diary.*

C 207

Barbara Delatiner, "Algren Entering the East End Ring," *New York Times*—Long Island supplement (26 April 1981), XXI-15.

Interview.

C 208

Janet Cawley, "Nelson Algren Remembered as Tough and Tender," *Chicago Tribune* (11 May 1981), 3.

Quotes Algren.

C 209

Jan Herman, " 'In' at Last: Nelson Algren's Final Happy Days," *Chicago Sun-Times Book Week* (17 May 1981), 1, 31.

Quotes Algren.

C 210
Robert Cromie, "Algren Had His Code, and It Got Him Arrested," *Chicago Tribune Book World* (17 May 1981), 1, 6.

Quotes Algren.

C 211
"Walk Pretty All the Way," *Chicago,* 30 (June 1981), 160–164.

Story.

C 212
Clancy Sigal, "Recalling the Kindness of Algren," *Los Angeles Times Book Review* (7 June 1981), 3.

Quotes Algren.

C 213
"So Long, Swede Risberg," *Chicago,* 30 (July 1981), 138–141, 158.

Article.

C 214
Wolf Wondratschek, "Algren, Wer?" *Literaturtip,* #1 (Herbst 1981), 45–46.

Quotes Algren in English and German.

C 215
"Calhoun," *Literaturtip,* #1 (Herbst 1981), 47–53.

Excerpt from *Calhoun.*

C 216
Saul Maloff, "The Time, The Space, The Quiet," *New York Times Book Review* (29 November 1981), 13, 40–41.

Quotes Algren.

C 217
"Searching for the Real Chicago," *Chicago,* 32 (January 1983), 125–127, 153–155.

Transcription of a 1957 symposium involving Frank Lloyd Wright, Rudolph Ganz, Archibald MacLeish, and Algren. See C 69.

C 218
Andrew Patner, "El Stop Isaiah," *haymarket literary supplement,* 3 (June 1983), 5–6.

Quotes Algren.

UNLOCATED CLIPPINGS

C 219
"WHERE I live: In front of a 16-inch TV screen . . . . " 1951.

Prepublication excerpt from *Chicago: City on the Make.*

C 220
Marjory Wood, "Algren Gives Writers' Group Views of Life."

Quotes Algren. Report of 1952 speech. See C 53.

C 221
"AUTHOR—After the screening I lunched at the Imperial House . . . . " 1955.

Quotes Algren.

C 222
"Nelson Algren Replies," *Chicago Tribune Magazine.*

Letter.

D. First Appearances of Reviews by Algren in Magazines and Newspapers

D 1

Review of *A World to Win* by Jack Conroy, *The Windsor Quarterly,* 3 (Fall 1935), 73.

D 2

Review of *Judgment Day* by James T. Farrell, *The Windsor Quarterly,* 3 (Fall 1935), 83–84.

D 3

"A World We Never Saw," *The Beacon* (November 1937), 20–21.

Review of *The Short Stories of James T. Farrell.*

D 4

"Sentiment with Terror," *Poetry,* 55 (December 1939), 157–159.

Review of *Collected Poems* by Robert Graves.

D 5

"Lloyd Frankenberg's Poems," *Poetry,* 56 (April 1940), 46–48.

Review of *The Red Kite* by Frankenberg.

D 6

"Fragmentary, Intense," *Poetry,* 57 (January 1941), 278–279.

Review of *Poems* by William Pillin.

D 7

"We Thank You with Reservations," *Poetry,* 59 (January 1942), 220–224.

Review of *I Went Into the Country* by Harry Roskolenko, *The Man on the Queue* by Sidney Alexander, and *We Thank You All the Time* by Norman Macleod.

D 8

"A Tale of Corn and Cotton in the Delta Country," *Chicago Sun* (6 September 1942), 30.

Review of *Dollar Cotton* by John Faulkner.

135

D 9

"A Beady Career Woman in Modern Manhattan," *Chicago Sun* (20 September 1942), 34.

Review of *A Time to Be Born* by Dawn Powell.

D 10

"North Atlantic Patrol In Hard Swift Story," *Chicago Sun* (18 October 1942), 21.

Review of *East of Farewell* by Howard Hunt.

D 11

"A Cinematic Novel of Life in the Carolinas," *Chicago Sun Book Week* (1 November 1942), 31.

Review of *Men of Albermarle* by Inglis Fletcher.

D 12

"From Locusts and Tax Collectors to the Happy Land," *Chicago Sun Book Week* (24 January 1943), 4.

Review of *Syrian Yankee* by Salom Rizk.

D 13

"A Social Poet," *Poetry,* 61 (February 1943), 634–636.

Review of *For My People* by Margaret Walker.

D 14

"A Joyous Frolic with Down-and-Outers," *Chicago Sun Book Week* (21 February 1943), 4.

Review of *Snow Above Town* by Donald Hough.

D 15

"Weariness, Danger and Pain: Subjective Report of a Writing Commando," *Chicago Sun Book Week* (14 March 1943), 5.

Review of *The Voice of the Trumpet* by Robert Henriques.

D 16

"Varying Viewpoints," *Poetry,* 63 (April 1943), 50–53.

Review of *Blind Dawn* by Stanley Kidder Wilson, *Fence of Fire* by Reitza Dine Wirtschafter, and *Rind of Earth* by August Derleth.

D 17

"Satire on a Labor Hating Uplifter," *Chicago Sun Book Week* (25 April 1943), 2.

Review of *Gideon Planish* by Sinclair Lewis.

D 18

"Heroic Army Doctor in Australia," *Chicago Sun Book Week* (2 May 1943), 6.

Review of *The Story of Doctor Wassell* by James Hilton.

D 19

"Cynical Ennui in an Ill-Timed Novel," *Chicago Sun Book Week* (9 May 1943), 6.

Review of *The Fifth Seal* by Mark Aldanov.

D 20

"DeVries' Humor Tempers This Novel of Pursuit," *Chicago Daily News* (30 June 1943), 19.

Review of *The Handsome Heart* by Peter DeVries.

D 21

"Magic and Melancholy," *Poetry,* 63 (October 1943), 52–55.

Review of *Lines for the Canonization of Pedro Domecq* by George Smedley Smith, *The Masculine Dead* by William Everson, and *Ten War Elegies* by Everson.

D 22

"Miner Minstrels," *Poetry,* 63 (November 1943), 106–108.

Review of *Coal Dust on the Fiddle* by George Korson.

D 23

"Right Guy in a Wrong World Battles a Finagling Society," *Chicago Daily News* (28 June 1944), 16.

Review of *The Rebellion of Leo McGuire* by Clyde Brion Davis.

D 24

"Human Horseplay and Horror in Erskine Caldwell Stories," *Chicago Daily News* (30 August 1944), 17.

Review of *Stories by Erskine Caldwell,* edited by Henry Seidel Canby.

D 25

"Three Against the World," *Poetry,* 65 (October 1944), 51–54.

Review of *Flight Above Cloud* by John Pudney, *Sailing or Drowning* by Allen Curnow, and *The Second Man* by Julian Symons.

D 26

"Erskine Caldwell's Horseplay Gets Out of Hand This Time," *Chicago Daily News* (18 October 1944), 18.

Review of *Tragic Ground* by Caldwell.

D 27
"Frontier History Takes on Semblance of a Road Show," *Chicago Daily News* (25 October 1944), 24.

Review of *Sun in Their Eyes* by Monte Barrett.

D 28
"When G.I. Joe Comes Home, Will He Fit as a Civilian?" *Chicago Daily News* (27 December 1944), 9.

Review of *They Dream of Home* by Niven Busch.

D 28a
"Prehistoric Man Battles Elements and His Own Mind," *Chicago Daily News* (3 January 1945), 13.

Review of *The Golden Rooms* by Vardis Fisher.

D 29
"Jet-Propelled Airliner Can't Save This Novel," *Chicago Daily News* (20 February 1946), 17.

Review of *Yeoman's Progress* by Douglas Reed.

D 30
"Aurora Borealis Announces Judgment Day in Kentucky," *Chicago Daily News* (20 March 1946), 21.

Review of *Foretaste of Glory* by Jesse Stuart.

D 31
"Strip Tease at Country Club with Murder for Dessert," *Chicago Daily News* (20 March 1946), 37.

Review of *Stag Night* by Philips Rogers.

D 32
"Small Things Turn Lyrical in Boy's Eyes," *Chicago Daily News* (10 April 1946), 3.

Review of *Blue Boy* by Jean Giono.

D 33
"Faint Heart Ne'er Won Lady in Prehistoric Days, Either," *Chicago Daily News* (17 April 1946), 19.

Review of *Intimations of Eve* by Vardis Fisher.

D 34
"Mulatto Family Struggles with Soil of North Dakota," *Chicago Daily News* (24 April 1946), 3.

Review of *American Daughter* by Era Bell Thompson.

D 35

"Literary Pen Balks Chance for Tragedy," *Chicago Daily News* (1 May 1946), 32.

Review of *The Lost Men* by Benedict Thielen.

D 36

"Nazis Rule in Belgium," *Chicago Daily News* (8 May 1946), 21.

Review of *Written in Darkness* by Anne Somerhausen.

D 37

"With Scruples as a Luxury: Timely Account of Trials of an Honest Labor Leader," *Chicago Sun Book Week* (24 November 1946), 27.

Review of *Angry Dust* by Dorothy Stockbridge.

D 38

"Tangled Lives in Tourist Camp: Flatfooted Philosophy Mars 'Suspense Story,' " *Philadelphia Inquirer Book Review* (16 February 1947), 5.

Review of *Double Image* by Arthur Herbert Bryant.

D 39

"Mass Misery of Puerto Rico: Destitution Described with Brutal Vividness," *Philadelphia Inquirer Book Review* (2 March 1947), 4.

Review of *The Fiesta at Anderson's House* by Scott Graham Williamson.

D 40

"Irish Folk Stories by Mary Lavin Show Deep Understanding," *Chicago Sun Book Week* (9 March 1947), 8.

Review of *At Sallygap and Other Stories* by Lavin.

D 41

"Romance on a Streamliner: A Professor Finds Love on a Transcontinental Train," *Philadelphia Inquirer Book Review* (16 March 1947), 6.

Review of *Three for Bedroom C* by Goddard Lieberson.

D 42

"Word-Etching of Teeming City Life," *Philadelphia Inquirer Book Review* (30 March 1947), 9.

Review of *Behold a Cry* by Alden Bland.

D 43

"Modern Music with Human Background," *Philadelphia Inquirer Book Review* (25 May 1947), 7.

Review of *Little Gate* by Annemarie Ewing.

D 44

"A Crofter's Son Sees Hope in Love of Land," *Philadelphia Inquirer Book Review* (1 June 1947), 6.

Review of *The Drinking Well* by Neil M. Gunn.

D 45

"Brooklyn's Slums in the Raw: A Sordid Picture of Adolescent Gangsterism," *Philadelphia Inquirer Book Review* (8 June 1947), 6.

Review of *The Amboy Dukes* by Irving Shulman.

D 46

"Mere Male in a Matriarchy: Our Hero Gropes Way Out of Maze of Taboos," *Philadelphia Inquirer Book Review* (8 June 1947), 9.

Review of *Adam and the Serpent* by Vardis Fisher.

D 47

"Blast at Materialistic Age: Addle-Headed Girl Pictured as Symbol of Lust," *Philadelphia Inquirer Book Review* (22 June 1947), 7.

Review of *Collision* by James Gordon.

D 48

"Germans Against Germans: A First-Hand Account of Shame at Buchenwald," *Philadelphia Inquirer Book Review* (20 July 1947), 6.

Review of *Forest of the Dead* by Ernst Wiechert.

D 49

"Johnny Comes Marching Home," *Philadelphia Inquirer Book Review* (17 August 1947), 4.

Review of *Blue City* by Kenneth Millar.

D 50

"Story of Dan and His Scarf Complex," *Philadelphia Inquirer Book Review* (31 August 1947), 6.

Review of *The Scarf* by Robert Bloch.

D 51

"Portrait of a Psychopathic Heel," *Philadelphia Inquirer Book Review* (7 September 1947), 4.

Review of *The Dead Tree Gives No Shelter* by Virgil Scott.

D 52

"Bandleader in Marital Trap," *Philadelphia Inquirer Book Review* (5 October 1947), 6.

Review of *Little Boy Blues* by George Willis.

D 53

Review of *Darker Grows the Valley* by Harry Harrison Kroll, *Chicago Sun Book Day* (13 October 1947), 29.

D 54

"Inner Conflict of Principled Bureaucrat," *Philadelphia Inquirer Book Review* (19 October 1947), 7.

Review of *But Not Yet Slain* by Benjamin Appel.

D 55

"Editor Finds No Man Is an Island," *Philadelphia Inquirer Book Review* (9 November 1947), 2.

Review of *Something Wonderful to Happen* by Darwin L. Teilhet.

D 56

"Dreiser's Despair Reaffirmed in 'The Stoic': He Blazed Literary Trail, Only to Find Dead-End He Had Predicted," *Philadelphia Inquirer Book Review* (23 November 1947), 3.

Review of *The Stoic* by Theodore Dreiser.

D 57

"Classics of Supernatural Leavened with High Humor," *Chicago Sun Book Week* (23 November 1947), 9.

Review of *Man Into Beast: Strange Tales of Transformation* by A. C. Spectorsky.

D 58

"Tragic Plight of Immigrants Told by Valtin," *Chicago Sun Book Week* (30 November 1947), 7.

Review of *Castle in the Sand* by Jan Valtin.

D 59

"Young Author's Novel Shows Great Wisdom," *Chicago Sun Book Week* (3 December 1947), 11A.

Review of *The Hound* by Frederic Morton.

D 60

"Harbor Watcher," *Philadelphia Inquirer Book Review* (21 December 1947), 8.

Review of *A View of the Harbour* by Elizabeth Taylor.

D 61

"Caught in a Human Web," *Philadelphia Inquirer Book Review* (4 January 1948), 2.

Review of *So Joined* by Harlow Estes.

D 62

Review of *Venus and the Voters* by Gwyn Thomas, *Chicago Sun Book Day* (7 January 1948), 20.

D 63

"Violet Eyes," *Philadelphia Inquirer Book Review* (18 January 1948), 4.

Review of *On Such a Night* by Anthony Quayle.

D 64

"For First Edition Collectors," *Chicago Sun and Times Book Day* (17 February 1948), 25.

Review of *The Light and the Dark* by C. P. Snow.

D 65

" 'Too Hard a World,' " *Chicago Sun-Times Book Day* (1 April 1948), 44.

Review of *Never Love a Stranger* by Harold Robbins.

D 66

"Success Measured in Distance from 12th St. to Wilson Ave.," *Chicago Sun-Times Book Week* (11 April 1948), 6.

Review of *Someday, Boy* by Sam Ross.

D 67

"North African Shadows," *Philadelphia Inquirer Book Review* (18 April 1948), 5.

Review of *I Never Saw an Arab like Him* by James A. Maxwell.

D 68

"Killer Diller," *Philadelphia Inquirer Book Review* (2 May 1948), 7.

Review of *Kiss Tomorrow Goodbye* by Horace McCoy.

D 69

"Is Love Enough?" *Chicago Sun-Times Book Day* (10 June 1948), 51.

Review of *The Edge of the Night* by John Prebble.

D 70

"Possums and Blackmail," *Chicago Sun-Times Book Day* (19 August 1948), 42.

Review of *This Very Earth* by Erskine Caldwell.

D 71

"German Army at Stalingrad," *Chicago Sun-Times Book Day* (28 October 1948), 50.

Review of *Stalingrad* by Theodor Plievier.

D 72

"Four Fugitives from Dr. Freud in a Jungle Blazing with Beauty," *Chicago Sun-Times Book Week* (31 October 1948), 8X.

Review of *Storm and Echo* by Frederic Prokosch.

D 73

"Guerrilla War in Old Judea," *Chicago Sun-Times Book Week* (28 November 1948), 9X.

Review of *My Glorious Brothers* by Howard Fast.

D 74

"Novel Has an Explosive Ending," *Chicago Sun-Times Book Day* (6 December 1948), 57.

Review of *A Convoy Through the Dream* by Scott Graham Williamson.

D 75

"Cynical Writer Gets No Praise," *Chicago Sun-Times Book Week* (30 January 1949), 6X.

Review of *The Mask of Wisdom* by Howard Clewes.

D 76

"A Highly Readable Business," *Chicago Sun-Times Book Day* (17 February 1949), 44.

Review of *The Price Is Right* by Jerome Weidman.

D 77

"Duke—Who Had to Belong or 'Get His Head Busted In,' " *Chicago Sun-Times Book Week* (20 March 1949), 8X.

Review of *Duke* by Hal Ellson.

D 78

"Neither Snow nor Sleet Can Keep This Tough from the Delicatessen," *Chicago Sun-Times Book Week* (10 April 1949), 8X.

Review of *Cry Tough* by Irving Shulman.

D 79

"Between Two Races," *Chicago Sun-Times Book Day* (20 April 1949), 56.

Review of *Alien Land* by Willard Savoy.

D 80

"Spiritual Victory of a Poet," *Chicago Sun-Times Book Day* (9 May 1949), 40.

Review of *Limbo Tower* by William Lindsay Gresham.

D 81

"Basement of a Soul," *The Saturday Review of Literature,* 32 (29 October 1949), 28.

Review of *The Darkness Below* by Frederic Morton.

D 82

"Boyhood in Cincinnati," *Chicago Sun-Times Book Day* (31 October 1949), 38.

Review of *The Big Cage* by Robert Lowry.

D 83

"Faulkner's Thrillers," *New York Times Book Review* (6 November 1949), 4.

Review of *Knight's Gambit* by William Faulkner.

D 84

"Americans Who Were Left Behind," *Chicago Sun-Times Book Week* (20 November 1949), p. 9X.

Review of *Sinners, Come Away* by Leon Wilson.

D 85

"Judge Gave These Stories a 'Bum Rap,' " *Chicago Sun-Times Book Week* (4 December 1949), 15.

Review of *Prize Stories of 1949: O. Henry Awards,* edited by Herschell Brickell.

D 86

"Sin and Sand," *The Saturday Review of Literature,* 32 (17 December 1949), 18, 26.

Review of *The Sheltering Sky* by Paul Bowles.

D 87

"War Crimes Prosecutor Convicts Self," *Chicago Sun-Times Book Day* (14 February 1950), 7.

Review of *The Vintage* by Anthony West.

D 88

"Lonely, Romantic Girl Trapped by Tenements," *Chicago Sun-Times Book Day* (7 March 1950), 5.

Review of *Captain's Beach* by Sigrid de Lima.

D 89

"Haunting, Masterly Novel of Soviet Prison Camp," *Chicago Sun-Times Book Week* (26 March 1950), 20.

Review of *The Tormentors* by Richard Cargoe.

D 90

"Battle of Britain," *New York Times Book Review* (9 April 1950), 16.

Review of *My Time. My Life* by George Camden.

D 91

"Saroyan Double-Decker," *New York Times Book Review* (23 April 1950), 4.

Review of *The Twin Adventures* by William Saroyan.

D 92

"Friendship of GI's in War Told in 'Soldier's Story,' " *Chicago Sun-Times Book Week* (30 April 1950), 9.

Review of *The Friend* by Perry Wolff.

D 93

"A Lion and a Tiger," *New York Times Book Review* (11 June 1950), 18.

Review of *In Search* by Meyer Levin.

D 94

"Child of Earth," *New York Times Book Review* (30 July 1950), 12.

Review of *He, the Father* by Frank Mlakar.

D 95

"By Candlelight," *New York Times Book Review* (13 August 1950), 22.

Review of *Here Comes a Candle* by Fredric Brown.

D 96

"Artist's Brood," *New York Times Book Review* (5 November 1950), 32.

Review of *The Uneasy Years* by Forrest Rosaire.

D 97

"Case Studies of Dreams," *The Saturday Review of Literature,* 33 (9 December 1950), 16.

Review of *An American Dream Girl* by James T. Farrell.

D 98

"Loneliest Is the Lover," *New York Times Book Review* (18 March 1951), 5.

Review of *Rock Wagram* by William Saroyan.

D 99

"Cardboard Racketeers," *New York Times Book Review* (20 May 1951), 19.

Review of *Little Men, Big World* by W. R. Burnett.

D 100
"Packer's Progress," *New York Times Book Review* (2 March 1952), 24.

Review of *The Chicago Story* by Ira Morris.

D 101
"Second . . . Not Third," *The Saturday Review,* 35 (21 June 1952), 37.

Review of *Chicago: The Second City* by A. J. Liebling.

D 102
"Carnival of Roguery," *New York Times Book Review* (27 July 1952), 19.

Review of *Barbarians in Our Midst: A History of Chicago Crime and Politics* by Virgil W. Peterson.

D 103
"Spoon-fed Universe," *The Saturday Review,* 35 (6 December 1952), 35.

Review of *The Golden Spike* by Hal Ellson.

D 104
"One More Octopus," *The Saturday Review,* 36 (3 January 1953), 57.

Review of *Caesar's Angel* by Mary Anne Amsbary.

D 105
"Record of a Sure Hand," *The Saturday Review,* 36 (7 March 1953), 27–28.

Review of *The Golden Watch* by Albert Halper.

D 106
"On the Way Up," *The Saturday Review,* 36 (2 May 1953), 32.

Review of *The Square Trap* by Irving Shulman.

D 107
"Jungle of Tenements," *The Saturday Review,* 36 (6 June 1953), 16.

Review of *The Pecking Order* by Mark Kennedy.

D 108
"Bitter Physics of the Deprived," *The Saturday Review,* 36 (4 July 1953), 20–21.

Review of *Duke* by Hal Ellson.

D 109
"Matters of Manhood," *The Saturday Review,* 36 (25 July 1953), 15.

Review of *Summer Street* by Hal Ellson.

D 110

"New Chicago Cantos," *The Saturday Review,* 36 (14 November 1953), 29.

Review of *The Face of Time* by James T. Farrell.

D 111

"City Against Itself," *The Nation,* 178 (13 February 1954), 135–136.

Review of *Big Bill of Chicago* by Lloyd Wendt and Herman Kogan, and of *Fabulous Chicago* by Emmett Dedmon.

D 112

"Takes Shine Off the Brass in Funny Story of Air Force," *Chicago Sun-Times Book Week* (3 October 1954), 4.

Review of *No Time for Sergeants* by Mac Hyman.

D 113

"Heartless Novel About Africa," *Chicago Sun-Times Book Week* (24 April 1955), 4.

Review of *Something of Value* by Robert Ruark.

D 114

"A Family That Ran Away," *New York Times Book Review* (21 August 1955), 4.

Review of *The Flight into Egypt* by Jean Bloch-Michel.

D 114a

"An Intimate Look at Dylan Thomas," *Chicago Sun-Times Book Week* (1 January 1956), 4.

Review of *Dylan Thomas in America by John Malcolm Brinnin.*

D 115

"Politics, Sociology with Irish Brogue," *Chicago Sun-Times Book Week* (5 February 1956), 4.

Review of *The Last Hurrah* by Edwin O'Connor.

D 115a

"A Fearsome Formula Fails to Make Political Point," *Chicago Sun-Times Book Week* (7 June 1956), 4.

Review of *The Ninth Wave* by Eugene Burdick.

D 116

"Lost Man," *The Nation,* 183 (1 December 1956), 484.

Review of *Giovanni's Room* by James Baldwin.

D 116a
"Author Follows Title, 'Makes Light of It,' " *Chicago Sun-Times Book Week* (7 January 1957), 6.

Review of *Make Light of It* by William Carlos Williams.

D 117
"Men Who Were Marked for Destruction," *New York Times Book Review* (17 March 1957), 4–5.

Review of *The Legion of the Damned* by Sven Hassel.

D 118
"Heroics in the Burmese Jungle," *Chicago Sun-Times Book Week* (24 March 1957), 6.

Review of *Never So Few* by Tom T. Chamales.

D 119
"The Stars Were for Hocking," *New York Times Book Review* (12 May 1957), 7.

Review of *The Magnificent Rube: The Life and Gaudy Times of Tex Rickard* by Charles Samuels.

D 120
"After the Gibbet, Uncle Billy Gets a Sympathetic Word," *Chicago Sun-Times Book Week* (26 May 1957), 6.

Review of *They Hanged My Saintly Billy* by Robert Graves.

D 121
"Kerouac Deftly Etches the 'Go' Generation," *Chicago Sun-Times Book Week* (8 September 1957), 4.

Review of *On the Road* by Jack Kerouac.

D 122
"Battling All the Way," *New York Times Book Review* (8 December 1957), 32.

Review of *No Man Stands Alone: The True Story of Barney Ross* by Barney Ross and Martin Abramson.

D 123
"He Writes with Lots of Heart," *Chicago Sun-Times Book Week* (26 January 1958), 4.

Review of *My Face for the World to See* by Alfred Hayes.

D 124
"8 'Angry Ones' Declare a British Existentialism," *Chicago Sun-Times Book Week* (13 April 1958), 1.

Review of *Declarations,* essays by Colin Wilson, John Osborne, John Wain, Kenneth Tynan, Bill Hopkins, Lindsay Anderson, Stuart Holroyd, and Doris Lessing.

D 125

"Author Bites Critic," *The Nation,* 187 (2 August 1958), 57.

Review of *Man in Modern Fiction* by Edmund Fuller.

D 126

"Epitaph Writ in Syrup," *The Nation,* 187 (16 August 1958), 78.

Review of *Let No Man Write My Epitaph* by Willard Motley. A slightly different version appears as "Motley Novel Tackles the Dope Problem," *Chicago Sunday Tribune Magazine of Books* (17 August 1958), 1–2.

D 127

"Robert Smith Tells Us Where We've Gone," *Chicago Sun-Times Book Week* (5 October 1958), 4.

Review of *Where He Went* by Robert Paul Smith. A slightly different version appears as "Passion or Piety," *The Nation,* 187 (8 November 1958), 346.

D 128

"Fabulous Firetrap," *The Saturday Review,* 41 (22 November 1958), 35.

Review of *The Great Chicago Fire* by Robert Cromie.

D 129

"Masonic Madness," *The Saturday Review,* 41 (13 December 1958), 36.

Review of *This Woman* by Pietro di Donato.

D 130

"The Sad Amphibia," *The Nation,* 188 (31 January 1959), 105–106.

Review of *The Sleep of Baby Filbertson and Other Stories* by James Leo Herlihy. A slightly different version appears as "Useless, Unzipped, Loveless, Defrauded," *Chicago Sun-Times Book Week* (1 February 1959), 4. See E 5.

D 131

"Old Fires," *The Nation,* 188 (28 March 1959), 280–281.

Review of *The Return* by Herbert Mitgang. A slightly different version appears as "Sulfurous Conflict on Sicilian Volcano," *Chicago Sun-Times Book Week* (29 March 1959), 4.

D 132

"Dreiser Letters Without Love," *Chicago Sun-Times Book Week* (10 May 1959), 6.

Review of *Letters of Theodore Dreiser,* edited by Robert H. Elias. A slightly different version appears as "Dreiser Hedged Out," *The Nation,* 188 (16 May 1959), 459–460.

D 133
"Chicago Review in an Anthology," *Chicago Sun-Times Book Week* (31 May 1959), 4.

Review of *Chicago Review Anthology,* edited by David Ray. A slightly different version appears as "No Lorgnette for Bessie," *The Nation,* 188 (27 June 1959), 580–581.

D 134
"Simone: A New Kind of Nun," *Chicago Sun-Times Book Week* (14 June 1959), 10.

Review of *Memoirs of a Dutiful Daughter* by Simone de Beauvoir.

D 135
"Wild Times of Big Spender—This Baby Packs a Satire," *Chicago Sun-Times Book Week* (21 February 1960), 4.

Review of *The Magic Christian* by Terry Southern. A slightly different version appears as "Making It Hot," *The Nation,* 189 (27 February 1960), 192–193. See E 10.

D 136
"Man with the Luger," *The Nation,* 192 (4 March 1961), 192–193.

Review of *Journey Not to End* by Paul Herr.

D 137
"Shared Corruption," *The Nation,* 192 (20 May 1961), 443.

Review of *The Coral Barrier* by Pierre Gascar.

D 138
"The Catch," *The Nation,* 193 (4 November 1961), 357–358.

Review of *Catch-22* by Joseph Heller. See B 32, E 3.

D 139
"Junkie Beware," *The Nation,* 194 (3 February 1962), 106.

Review of *The Drug Experience,* edited by David Ebin.

D 140
"Nothing Is Really Left Behind," *New York Times Book Review* (18 February 1962), 4–5.

Review of *Going Away: A Report, A Memoir* by Clancy Sigal.

D 141
"Ride on an Elephant," *The Nation,* 194 (19 May 1962), 449–450.

Review of *Contemporaries* by Alfred Kazin.

D 142
"A Resolve to Do His Dancing at the Waldorf Yet Remember the Stompers at the Savoy," *New York Herald Tribune: Books* (14 April 1963), 8.

Review of *And Then We Heard the Thunder* by John Oliver Killens.

D 143
"When that Town Really Toddled," *New York Herald Tribune: Books* (18 August 1963), 5.

Review of *Gaily, Gaily* by Ben Hecht.

D 144
"What Happened?" *The Nation,* 197 (14 December 1963), 422–423.

Review of *A Singular Man* by J. P. Donleavy.

D 145
"The Ginger Man Who Couldn't," *The Nation,* 198 (6 April 1964), 351–352.

Review of *Jubb* by Keith Waterhouse.

D 146
"Un-American Idea: Sex Can Be Funny," *Life,* 56 (8 May 1964), 8.

Review of *Candy* by Terry Southern.

D 147
"The Donkeyman by Twilight," *The Nation,* 198 (18 May 1964), 509–512.

Review-essay on novels by Terry Southern.

D 148
"Who's Who at the Lost & Found," *The Nation,* 198 (1 June 1964), 560–561.

Review of *A Moveable Feast* by Ernest Hemingway.

D 149
"Nobody Ever Takes the Sandwich," *Chicago Sun-Times Book Week* (14 June 1964), 6.

Review of *The Junkie Priest: Father Daniel Egan, S.A.* by John D. Harris, and of *The Protectors* by Harry S. Anslinger and J. Dennis Gregory.

D 150
"The Radical Innocent," *The Nation,* 199 (21 September 1964), 142–143.

Review-essay on novels by Bruce Jay Friedman.

D 151
"The Question of Simone de Beauvoir," *Harper's,* 230 (May 1965), 134, 136.

Review of *Force of Circumstance* by Beauvoir.

D 152
"His Ice-Cream Cone Runneth Over," *New York Herald Tribune Book Week* (16 May 1965), 5, 13.

Review of *Desolation Angels* by Jack Kerouac.

D 153
"Simone a Go Go," *Ramparts,* 4 (October 1965), 65–67.

Review of *Force of Circumstance* by Simone de Beauvoir.

D 154
"Raising Cain in the Corn Field," *New York Herald Tribune Book Week* (31 October 1965), 4, 33.

Review of *With the Procession* by Henry B. Fuller, *Windy McPherson's Son* by Sherwood Anderson, and *Gullible's Travels, Etc.* by Ring Lardner.

D 155
"Tear 'em Up, Friskybits," *New York Herald Tribune Book Week* (16 January 1966), 17.

Review of *I Jan Cremer* by Cremer.

D 156
"Close Call," *New York Herald Tribune Book Week* (6 February 1966), 12.

Review of *My Escape from the CIA* by Hughes Rudd.

D 157
"The Trouble at Gringo Gulch," *Chicago Sun-Times Book Week* (16 March 1966), 5, 15.

Review of *Let Noon Be Fair* by Willard Motley.

D 158
"Alex Never Saw the Bear," *New York Times Book Review* (12 June 1966), 30–31.

Review of *Orpheus on Top* by Edward Stewart.

D 159
"It's a Gay and Dreary Life," *The Critic,* 26 (August–September 1967), 67–68.

Review of *Eustace Chisholm and the Works* by James Purdy.

D 160

"Five Novels in One," *The Critic*, 26 (October–November 1967), 77–78.

Review of *The Upper Hand* by John William Corrington.

D 161

"Between Dream and Waking," *The Critic*, 26 (December 1967–January 1968), 71–72.

Review of *A Story That Ends with a Scream and Eight Others* by James Leo Herlihy.

D 162

"Waiting for Golda," *The Critic*, 26 (April–May 1968), 78–79.

Review of *The Tower of Babel* by Morris West.

D 163

"Native Son," *The Critic*, 26 (June–July 1968), 66–67.

Review of *Richard Wright* by Constance Webb.

D 164

"Sashaying Around," *The Critic*, 27 (October–November 1968), 86–87.

Review of *Tell Me How Long the Train's Been Gone* by James Baldwin.

D 165

"Texarkana Phantoms," *The Critic*, 27 (April–May 1969), 82–84.

Review of *A Time and a Place* by William Humphrey.

D 166

"No Ashes in the Urn," *The Critic*, 28 (January–February 1970), 84–86.

Review of *Travels with My Aunt* by Graham Greene.

D 167

"Imaginary Pockets," *The Nation*, 210 (30 March 1970), 376, 378.

Review of *Hard Times: An Oral History of the Great Depression* by Studs Terkel.

D 168

"Wake the Living," *The Critic*, 28 (March–April 1970), 74–76.

Review of *The Price of My Soul* by Bernadette Devlin.

D 169

"Tricky Dickey," *The Critic*, 28 (May–June 1970), 77–79.

Review of *Deliverance* by James Dickey.

D 170

"Original and One," *The Critic,* 29 (September–October 1970), 86–88.

Review of *City Life* by Donald Barthelme, and of *Land of a Million Elephants* by Asa Baber.

D 171

"A Guy Who Got Wiped," *Chicago Free Press,* 1 (16 November 1970), 32–33.

Review of *Blue Movie* by Terry Southern.

D 172

Review of *Bech: A Book* by John Updike, *The Critic,* 29 (November–December 1970), 84–86.

D 173

"Journal of 80s Holds Mirror to the 70s," *Los Angeles Times Book Review* (28 March 1971), 1, 4, 8.

Review of *Meeting the Bear: A Journal of the Black Wars* by Lloyd Zimpel.

D 174

Review of *Boss: Richard J. Daley of Chicago* by Mike Royko, *The Critic,* 29 (May–June 1971), 72–75. See E 9.

D 175

"Brendan Behan: A Wearer of the Mob's Mask," *Los Angeles Times Book Review* (27 June 1971), 1, 6, 11, 13.

Review of *Brendan* by Ulick O'Connor.

D 176

Review of *Way Uptown in Another World* by Shane Stevens, *Rolling Stone,* no. 87 (22 July 1971), 44.

D 177

Review of *The Long Walk at San Francisco State* by Kay Boyle, and of *The Merry Month of May* by James Jones, *The Critic,* 29 (July–August 1971), 68–70.

D 178

Review of *A Peep into the Twentieth Century* by Christopher Davis, *The Critic,* 30 (January–February 1972), 72–74, 76–77.

D 178a

"The Day They Penned Up Their Yellow Neighbors," *Los Angeles Times Book Review* (27 February 1972), 1, 12.

Review of *Executive Order 9066: The Internment of 110,000 Japanese-Americans* by Maisie and Richard Conrat.

D 179

"How to Break Silence Conspiracy Over Old Age," *Los Angeles Times Book Review* (25 June 1972), 1, 13, 15.

Review of *The Coming of Age* by Simone de Beauvoir.

D 180

Review of *Ringolevio: A Life Played for Keeps* by Emmett Grogan, *The Critic*, 31 (September–October 1972), 87–90.

D 181

Review of *The World of Apples* by John Cheever, *Chicago Tribune Book World* (13 May 1973), 1, 3.

D 182

"A Convocation of Vonnegut Characters," *Los Angeles Times Book Review* (10 June 1973), 3, 32.

Review of *Breakfast of Champions* by Kurt Vonnegut, Jr.

D 183

"The Great Hemorrhoid Hunt or *Kiss-Kiss Bang-Bang Goes Arty-Arty*," *The Critic*, 31 (July–August 1973), 6–7, 78–79.

Review of *Last Tango in Paris* (movie).

D 184

"An Unwilling Suspension of Disbelief," *Los Angeles Times Calendar* (16 September 1973), 20, 25.

Review of *Dead City* by Shane Stevens.

D 185

Review of *Holy Man: Father Damien of Molokai* by Gaven Daws, *The Critic*, 32 (November–December 1973), 76–83.

D 186

"Traveling a No Man's Land in the War Between the Races," *Los Angeles Times Book Review* (24 February 1974), 1–2, 9–11.

Review of *The Unfinished Quest of Richard Wright* by Michel Fabre.

D 187

"Get *All* the Money," *The Critic*, 32 (March–April 1974), 54–56.

Review of *The Exorcist* (movie).

D 188

"Life Deals from Bottom of Deck in Gambling Saga," *Los Angeles Times Calendar* (14 April 1974), 54–55.

Review of *Paradise Road* by David Scott Milton.

D 189
Review of *Malcolm Lowry: A Biography* by Douglas Day, *The Critic*, 32 (May–June 1974), 63–66.

D 190
"The Lesser Gatsby," *The Critic*, 32 (July–August–September 1974), 54–57.

Review of *The Great Gatsby* (movie).

D 191
"Tombstones, Architectural and Otherwise," *Los Angeles Times Book Review* (13 October 1974), 1, 8.

Review of *Eight Mortal Ladies Possessed* by Tennessee Williams.

D 192
Review of *Something Happened* by Joseph Heller, *The Critic*, 33 (October–November–December 1974), 90–91.

D 193
Review of *How Many Miles to Babylon?* by Jennifer Johnston, *The Critic*, 33 (January–February 1975), 66–67.

D 194
Review of *A Fan's Notes* and *Pages from a Cold Island* by Frederick Exley, *The Critic*, 34 (Fall 1975), 80–82.

D 195
"Celebrating the Duke: Ralph Gleason's Jazz Legacy," *Chicago Daily News Panorama* (25–26 October 1975), 2–3.

Review of *Celebrating the Duke: And Louis, Bessie, Bird, Carmen, Miles, Dizzy and Other Heroes* by Ralph Gleason.

D 196
"Uptown's Underside: A Grim Novel," *Chicago Daily News Panorama* (10–11 January 1976), 6.

Review of *City Dogs* by William Brashler.

D 197
"The Furious Grace of Garcia Marquez," *Chicago Daily News Panorama* (30–31 October 1976), 7, 10.

Review of *The Autumn of the Patriarch* by Gabriel García Márquez.

D 198
"Otto Preminger: Man with the Golden Prerogative," *Los Angeles Times West View* (15 May 1977), 3.

Review of *Preminger* by Preminger. Slightly revised as "Hollywood—Algren Remembers Preminger . . . , " *The Washington Book Review,* 1 (April 1979), 1, 10.

D 199

"The Hollow Tragicomedy That Was Ring Lardner's Life," *Chicago Tribune Book World* (7 August 1977), 1, 3.

Review of *Ring: A Biography of Ring Lardner* by Jonathan Yardley.

D 200

"A Bloody Humorist on the Warpath," *Chicago Tribune Book World* (12 February 1978), 2.

Review of *The Lady from Boston* by Tom McHale.

D 201

"Hemingway: His Misadventures with Fitzgerald," *Chicago Tribune Book World* (2 April 1978), 5F.

Review of *Scott and Ernest* by Matthew J. Bruccoli. Reprinted as "Nelson Algren on 'Scott and Ernest,' " *The Washington Book Review,* 1 (May 1979), 16, 12.

D 202

"Magician's Image of Reality," *Chicago Tribune Book World* (25 June 1978), 1, 6.

Review of *Innocent Erendira and Other Stories* by Gabriel García Márquez.

D 203

"Tinsel and Fool's Gold from Mario Puzo," *Chicago Tribune Book World* (24 September 1978), 7.

Review of *Fools Die* by Puzo. Slightly revised and expanded as "Nelson Algren on Mario Puzo," *The Washington Book Review*—unlocated.

D 204

"Motley: He Was an 'Invisible Man' Among Black Writers," *Chicago Tribune Book World* (25 February 1979), 1.

Review of *The Diaries of Willard Motley,* edited by Jerome Klinkowitz.

D 205

"Of Wine, Women, and Song," *Washington Post Book Week* (16 September 1979), 8.

Review of *The Intricate Music* by Thomas Kiernan, and of *Steinbeck and Covici* by Thomas Fensch.

D 206
"Hemingway's Poetry Shows Papa with his Bones Picked Clean," *Chicago Tribune Book World* (11 November 1979), 1, 14.

Review of *88 Poems by Ernest Hemingway,* edited by Nicholas Gerogiannis.

D 207
"The Liberating Vision of Richard Wright," *Chicago Tribune Book World* (8 June 1980), 3, 11.

Review of *Richard Wright: Ordeal of a Native Son* by Addison Gayle, Jr.

UNLOCATED CLIPPINGS

D 208
"Tangled Past Causes Scandal."

Review of *Never the Same Again* by Gerald Tesch. 1956.

D 209
"A Prix Goncourt Novel."

Review of *The Mercy of God* by Jean Cau. 1963.

D 210
"Gleason Report on Mayor Daley."

Review of *Daley of Chicago* by William F. Gleason. 1970.

D 211
"Women on Drugs: A Survivor's Tale."

Review of *Strong at the Broken Places: Women Who Have Survived Drugs* by Barbara Kerr. 1974.

D 212
"Islanders Surrounded by Loose Ends," *Los Angeles Times.*

Review of *Guerrillas* by V. S. Naipaul. 1975.

D 213
"Neither Good Grammar nor Good Taste," *Los Angeles Times.*

Review of *Sneaky People* by Thomas Berger. 1975.

D 214
"Reading the Anglo-Saxon Heart."

Review of *A Dream Journey* by James Hanley. 1976.

E. Blurbs

Statements written by Algren to promote works by other authors, arranged alphabetically by the authors' names.

E 1

Don DeLillo, *Americana* (New York: Pocket Books, 1973), #78321.

Blurb on first page.

E 2

Joyce Gourfain, *Dust Under the Rug* (New York: Pageant Press, 1952).

Statement in ad: *Chicago Daily News* (17 December 1952), 42.

E 3

Joseph Heller, *Catch-22* (New York: Simon & Schuster, [   ]).

Excerpt from review on dust jacket of first-edition reprinting. Also on front wrapper of Dell #1120 (1962). Also on dust jacket for 1966 Modern Library reprinting. See B 32, D 138.

E 4

James Leo Herlihy, *All Fall Down* (New York: Dutton, 1960).

Blurb on dust jacket.

E 5

James Leo Herlihy, *The Sleep of Baby Filbertson and Other Stories* (New York: Dutton, 1959).

Blurb on dust jacket. See D 130.

E 6

John Clellon Holmes, *Nothing More to Declare* (New York: Dutton, 1967).

Blurb on dust jacket.

E 7

Meridel Le Sueur, *Salute to Spring* (New York: International, 1940).

Blurb on dust jacket.

E 8

Paride Rombi, *Perdu* (New York: Harper, 1954).

Blurb on dust jacket.

161

E 9
Mike Royko, *Boss: Richard J. Daley of Chicago* (New York: Dutton, 1971).

Statement in ad: *Book World,* 5 (28 March 1971), 72. See D 174.

E 10
Terry Southern, *The Magic Christian* (New York: Bantam, 1964), #H2917.

Blurb on back wrapper. See D 135.

E 11
Lou Willett Stanek, *A Study Guide to Studs Terkel's Working* (New York: Avon, 1975?).

Blurb on front wrapper.

E 12
Studs Terkel, *Division Street: America* (New York: Pantheon, 1967).

Blurb on dust jacket.

E 13
Kurt Vonnegut, Jr., *God Bless You, Mr. Rosewater, or Pearls Before Swine* (New York, Chicago & San Francisco: Holt, Rinehart & Winston, 1965).

Blurb on dust jacket. Repeated on dust jacket for Vonnegut's *Mother Night* (New York: Harper and Row, 1966).

Appendices / Index

Appendix 1

Compiler's Notes

1. In 1959 Pennington Press announced *The World of Nelson Algren* by Arthur Shay and Algren. The book was not published. The publisher's catalogue is at the Thomas Cooper Library, University of South Carolina.

2. In 1963 Bernard Geis announced *Another Wild Walk with Nelson Algren* for September. The book was not published.

3. James Blake's *The Joint* (Garden City, N.Y.: Paris Review Editions/Doubleday, 1971) includes Blake's letters to Algren.

4. An ad for *Sanctuary* magazine in the January–February 1935 issue of *The Partisan Review* lists Algren among the contributors; no copy of *Sanctuary* has been located.

5. Algren was listed as an "Associate" in *The Partisan Review,* February–June 1936; and as a "Contributing Editor" in *Contact,* October 1960–September 1961.

6. *Ex Libris Nelson Algren.* [Chicago]: Trunk Line, [1975]. Xeroxed list of Algren's papers to be sold at auction.

Appendix 2

Books and Bibliographical Articles About Algren

Cox, Martha Heasley and Wayne Chatterton. *Nelson Algren.* Boston: Twayne, [1975].

Garon, Paul. "Nelson Algren in Paperback: A Checklist," *Paperback Quarterly,* 5 (Winter 1982), 50–60.

McCollum, Kenneth G. *Nelson Algren   A Checklist.* Detroit: Bruccoli Clark/ Gale Research, 1973.

Ploch, R. A. *Nelson Algren   Samuel Beckett.* [Columbus]: Ohio State University Libraries, 1966. Exhibition catalogue.

Studing, Richard. "A Nelson Algren Checklist," *Twentieth-Century Literature,* 19 (January 1973), 27–39.

———. "Researching and Collecting Nelson Algren," *American Book Collector,* 3 (January/February 1982), 32–37.

Index

Pittsburgh Series in Bibliography